EASY PIANO

YESTERDAY

MUSIC FROM THE ORIGINAL MOTION PICTURE SOUNDTRACK

ISBN 978-1-5400-6406-6

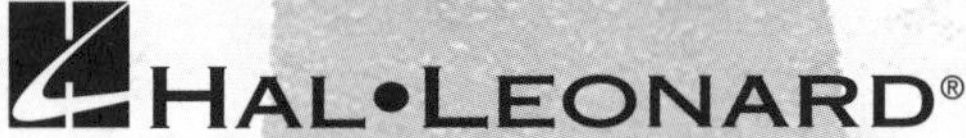

Visit Hal Leonard Online at
www.halleonard.com

Contact us:
Hal Leonard
7777 West Bluemound Road
Milwaukee, WI 53213
Email: info@halleonard.com

In Europe, contact:
Hal Leonard Europe Limited
42 Wigmore Street
Marylebone, London, W1U 2RN
Email: info@halleonardeurope.com

In Australia, contact:
Hal Leonard Australia Pty. Ltd.
4 Lentara Court
Cheltenham, Victoria, 3192 Australia
Email: info@halleonard.com.au

ALL YOU NEED IS LOVE

Words and Music by JOHN LENNON
and PAUL McCARTNEY

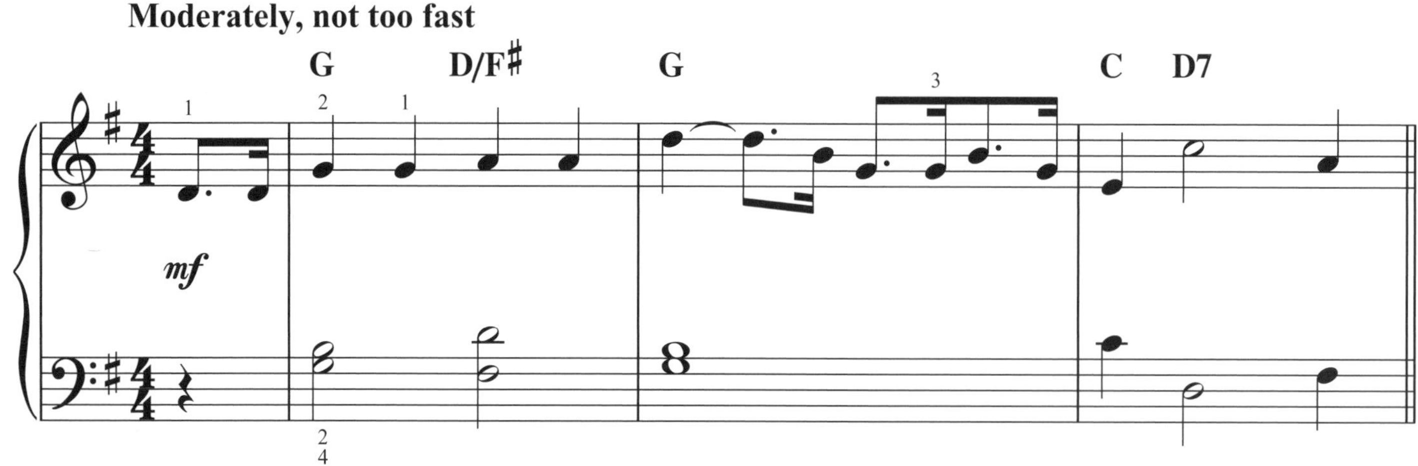

G
D/F♯
Em
There's noth - ing you can do that can't be done.
Noth - ing you can make that can't be made.
Noth - ing you can know that is - n't known.

G
D/F♯
Em
Noth - ing you can sing that can't be sung.
No one you can save that can't be saved.
Noth - ing you can see that is - n't shown.

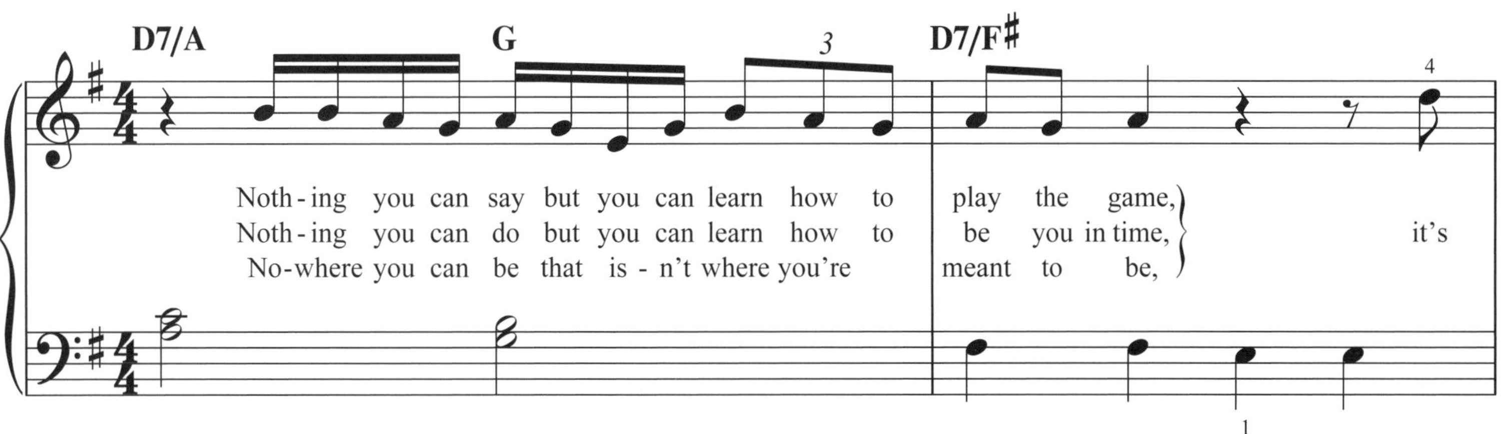
D7/A
G
D7/F♯
Noth - ing you can say but you can learn how to play the game,
Noth - ing you can do but you can learn how to be you in time,
No - where you can be that is - n't where you're meant to be,
it's

D7
1.
N.C.
2., 3.
N.C.
eas - y.

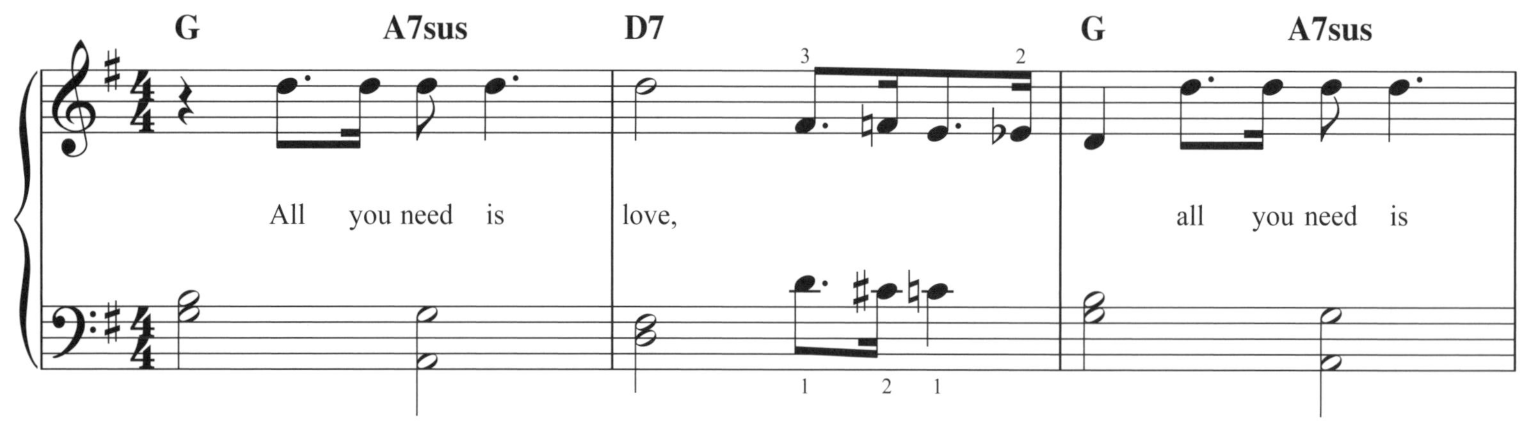
G
A7sus
D7
G
A7sus
All you need is
love,
all you need is

D7
G
B7/F#
Em
G/D
love,
all you need is
love, love,

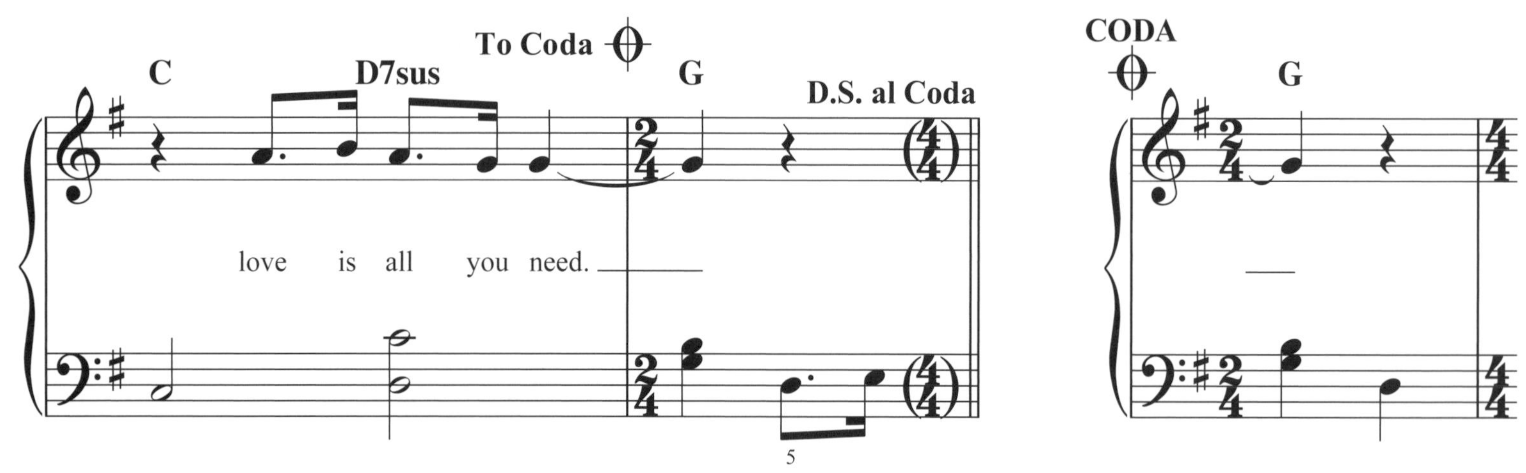
To Coda
C
D7sus
G
D.S. al Coda
CODA
G
love is all you need.

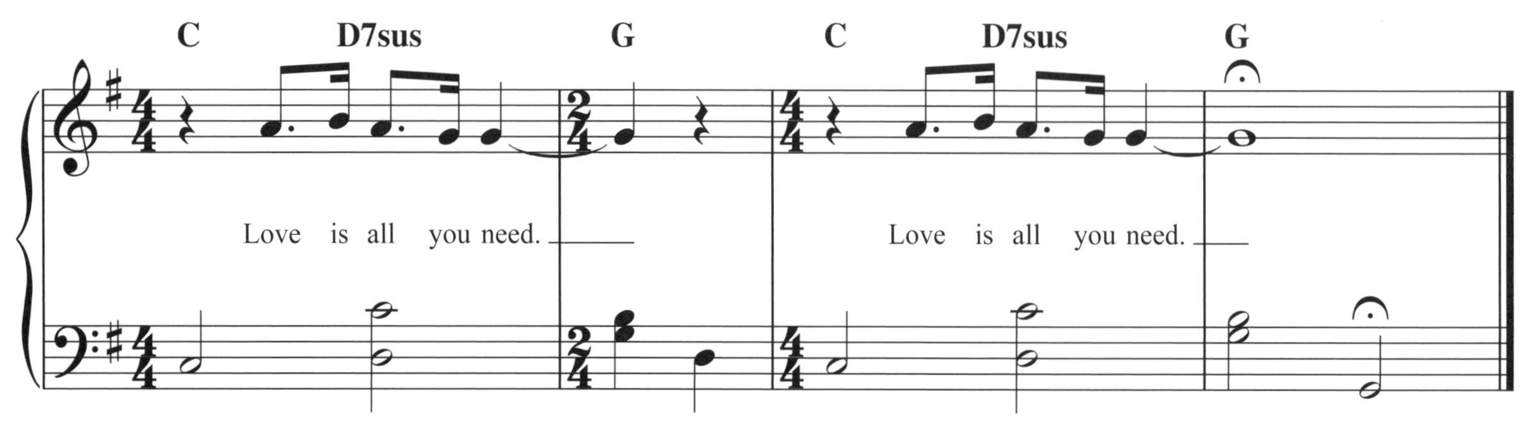
C
D7sus
G
C
D7sus
G
Love is all you need.
Love is all you need.

BACK IN THE U.S.S.R.

Words and Music by JOHN LENNON
and PAUL McCARTNEY

C
D
A
man, I had a dread-ful flight.
hon - ey, dis - con - nect the phone.
come and keep your com-rade warm.
I'm back in the U. S. S. R.,
3

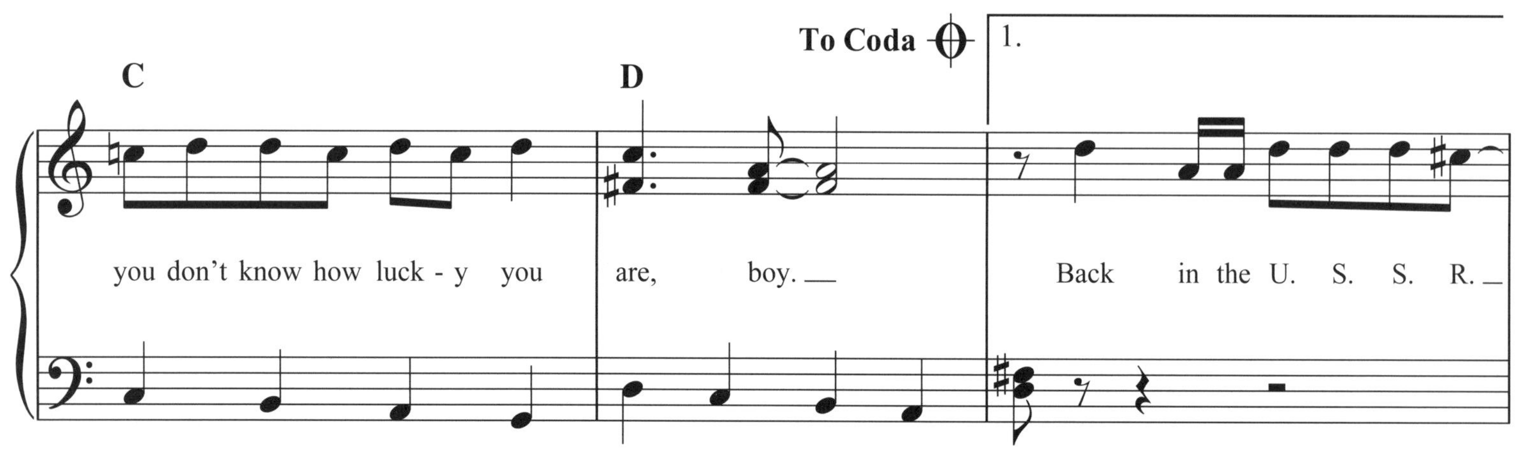
To Coda
1.
C
D
you don't know how luck - y you are, boy.
Back in the U. S. S. R.

2.
A
D E♭ E
D/E
Back in the U. S.,
back in the U. S.,
3

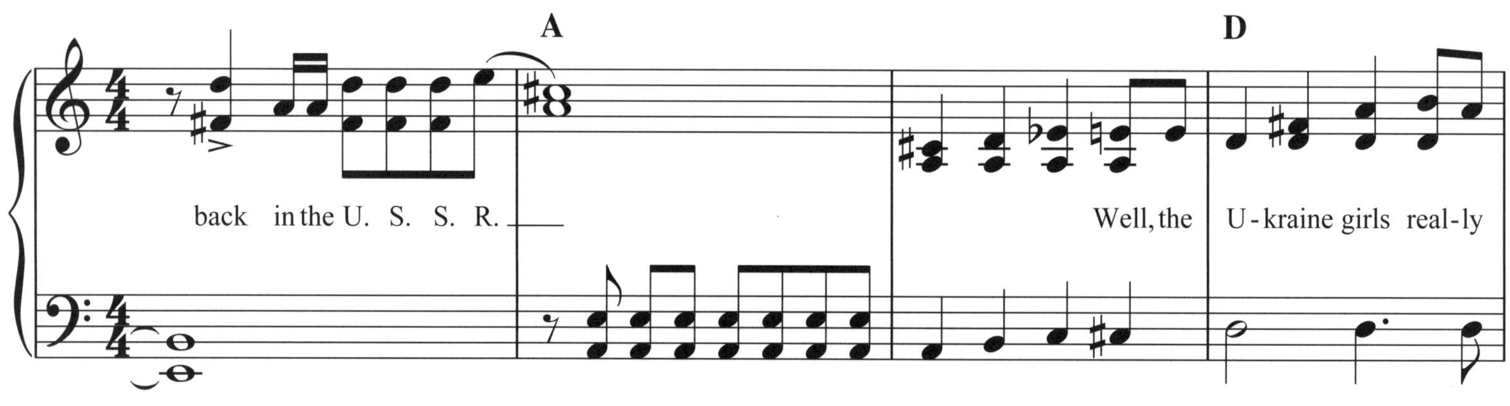
A
D
back in the U. S. S. R.
Well, the
U - kraine girls real - ly

A
D
F♯m/C♯
knock me out. They leave the West be - hind. And Mos - cow girls make me

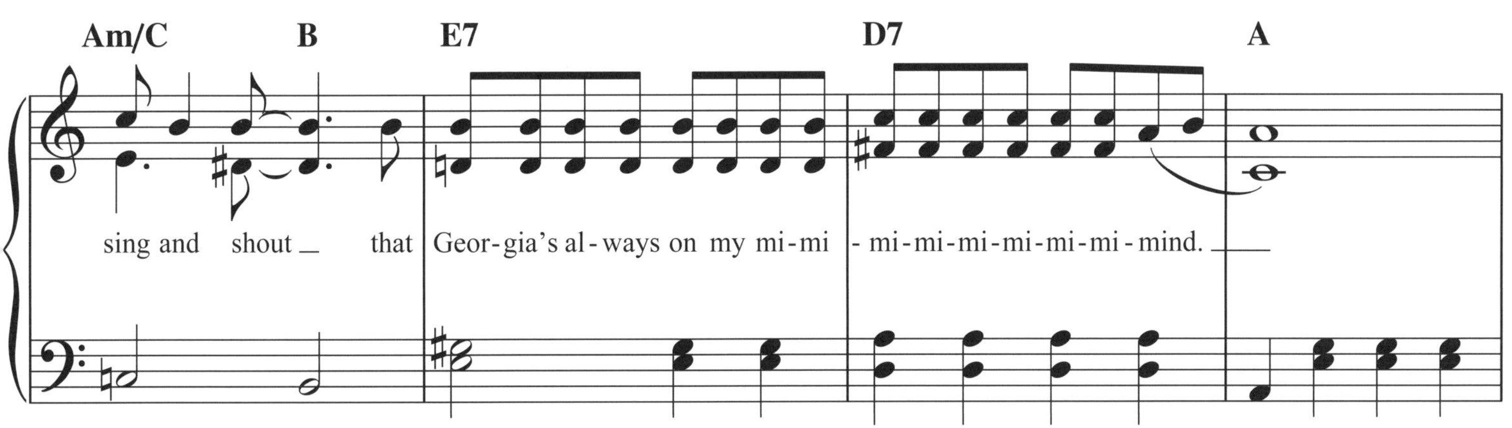
Am/C
B
E7
D7
A
sing and shout that Geor-gia's al-ways on my mi-mi - mi-mi-mi-mi-mi-mi-mind.

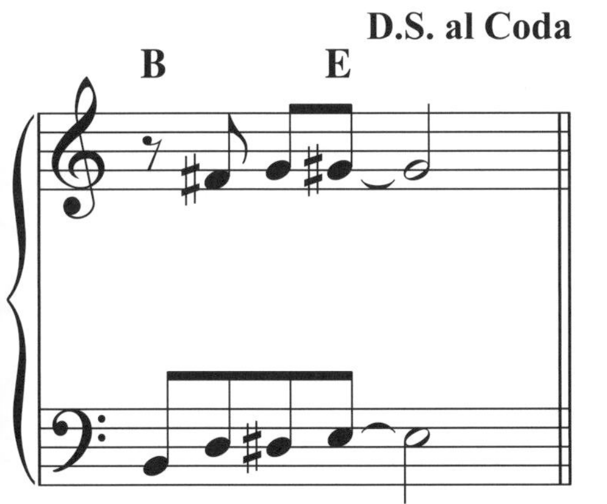
D.S. al Coda
B
E

CODA
A
Back in the U. S. S. R.

D E♭ E
A
Play 4 times
3

CARRY THAT WEIGHT

Words and Music by JOHN LENNON
and PAUL McCARTNEY

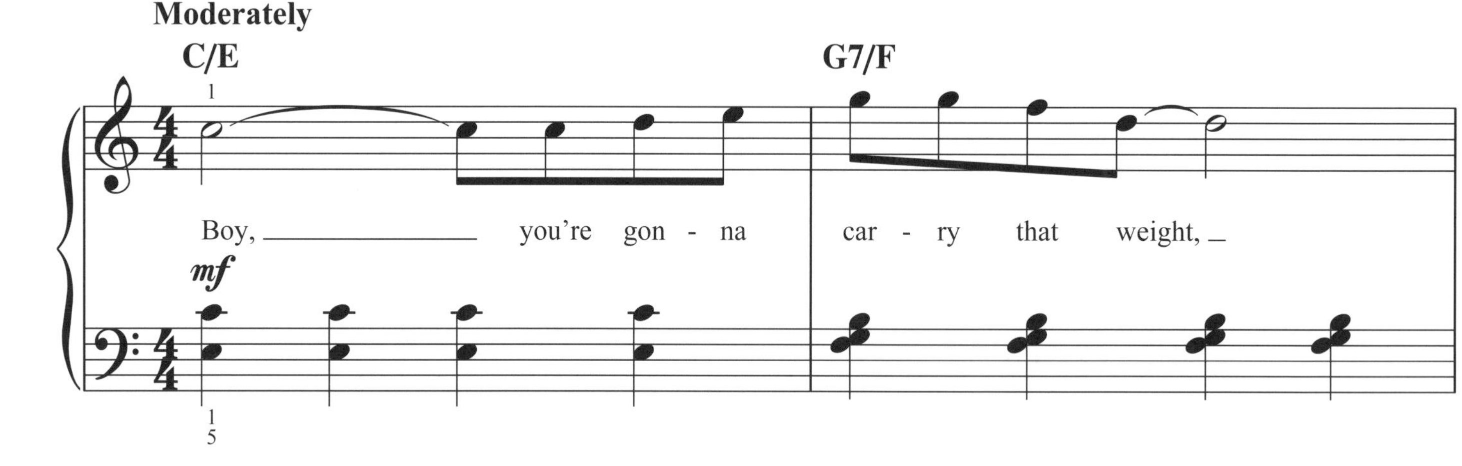

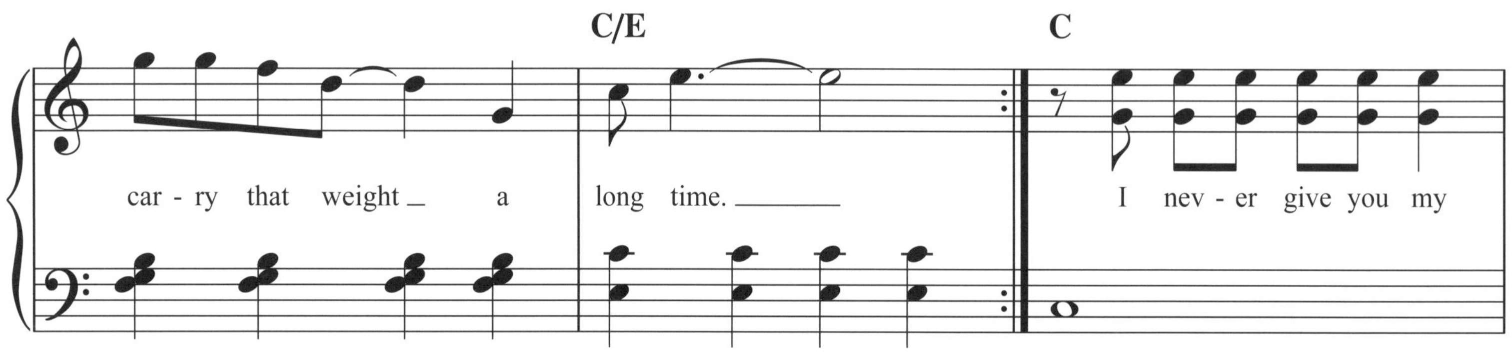

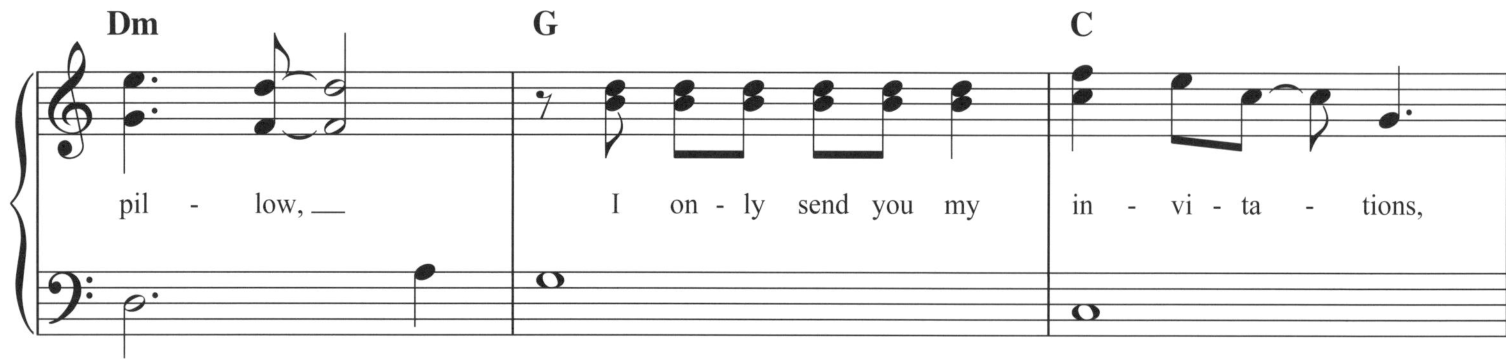

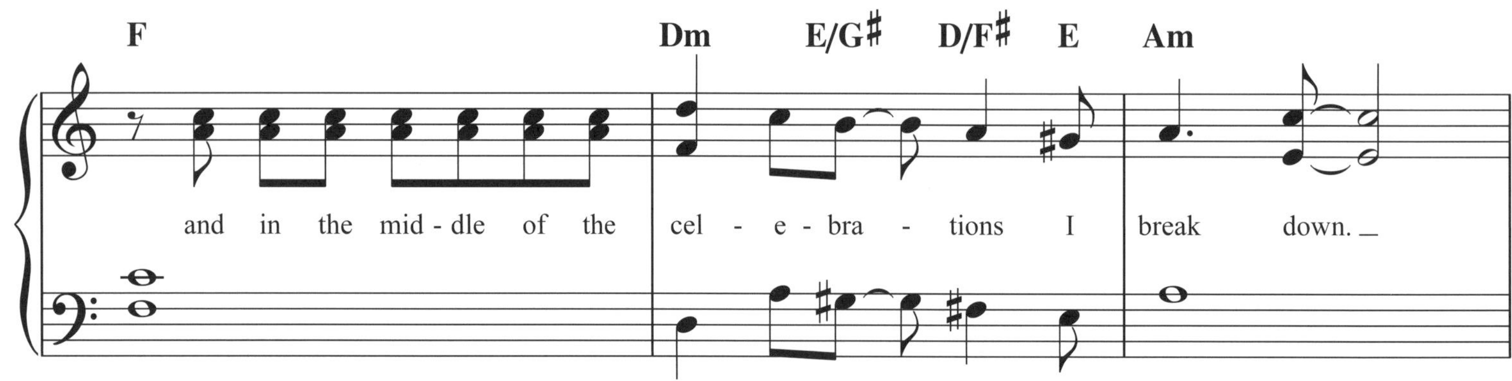

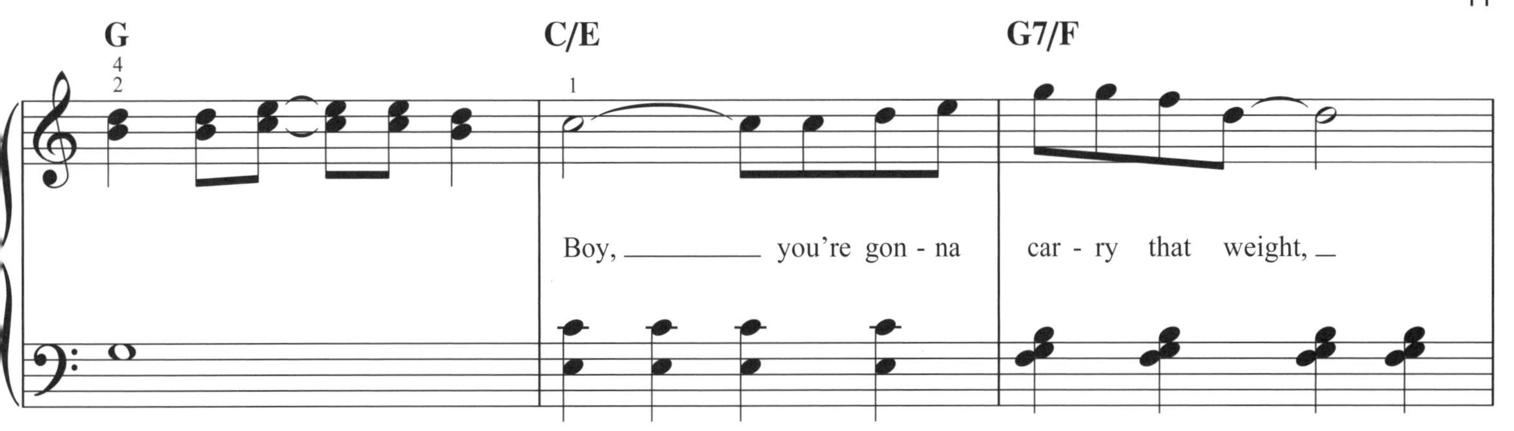
G
C/E
G7/F
4
2
1
Boy, you're gon - na
car - ry that weight,

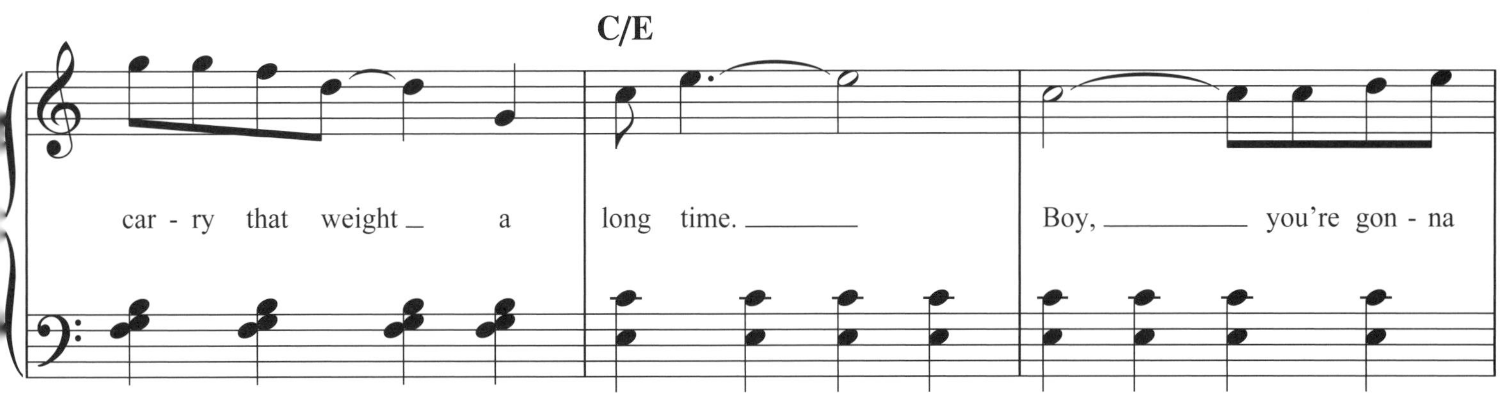
C/E
car - ry that weight a
long time.
Boy, you're gon - na

G7/F
C
G/B
car - ry that weight,
car - ry that weight a
long time.

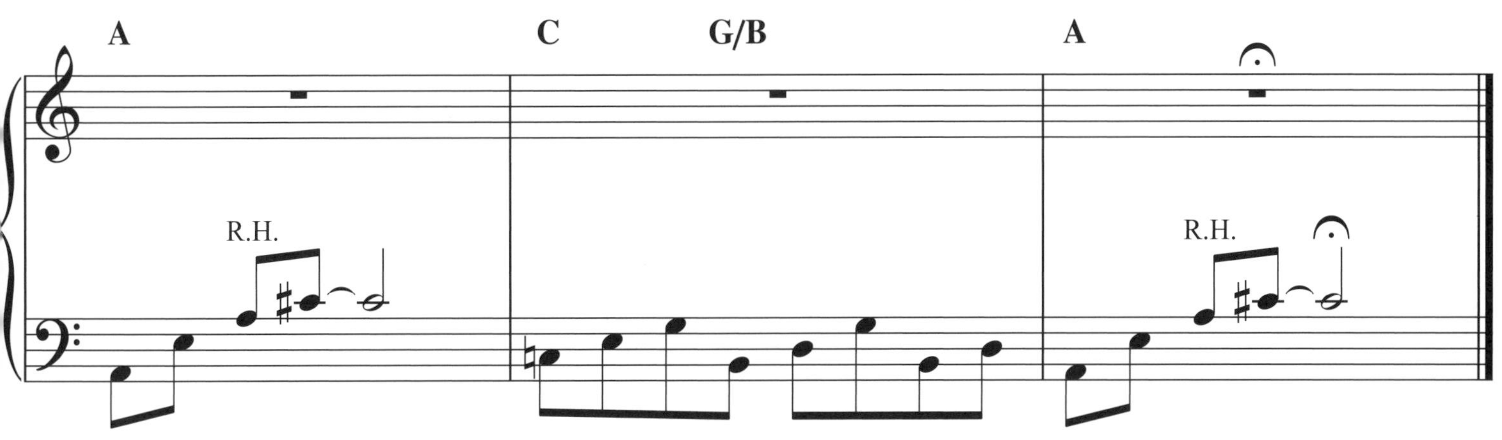
A
C
G/B
A
R.H.
R.H.

A HARD DAY'S NIGHT

Words and Music by JOHN LENNON
and PAUL McCARTNEY

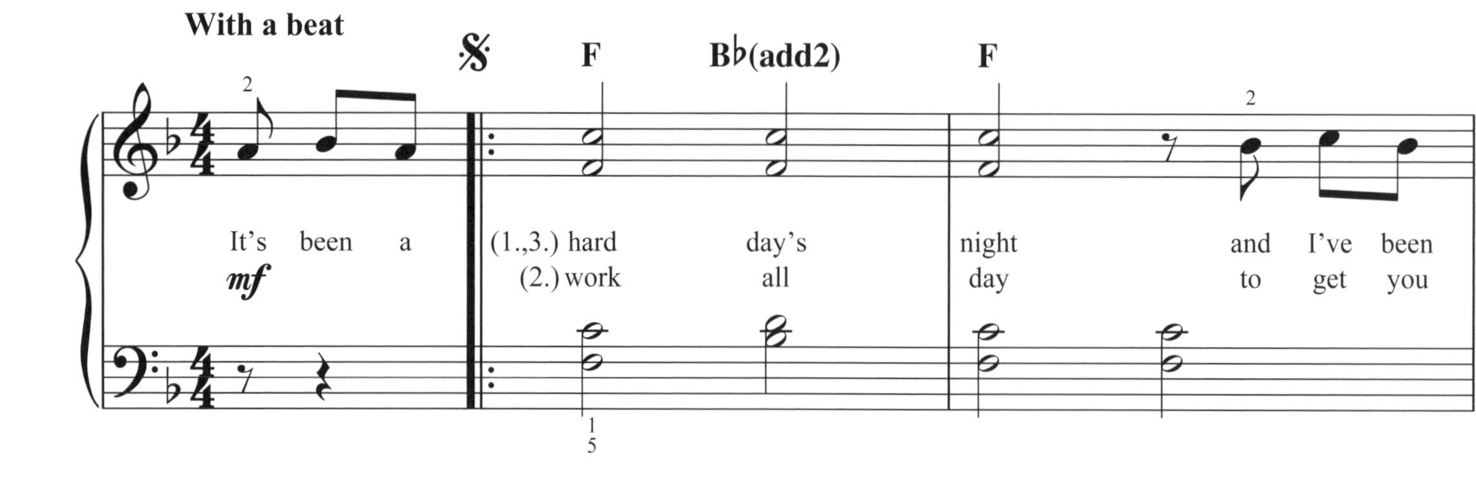

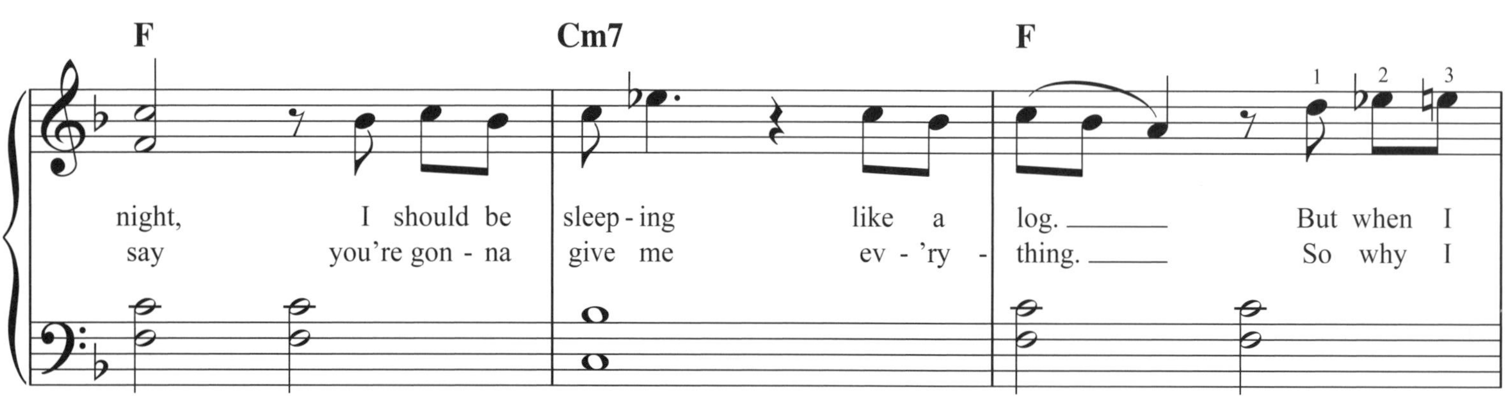

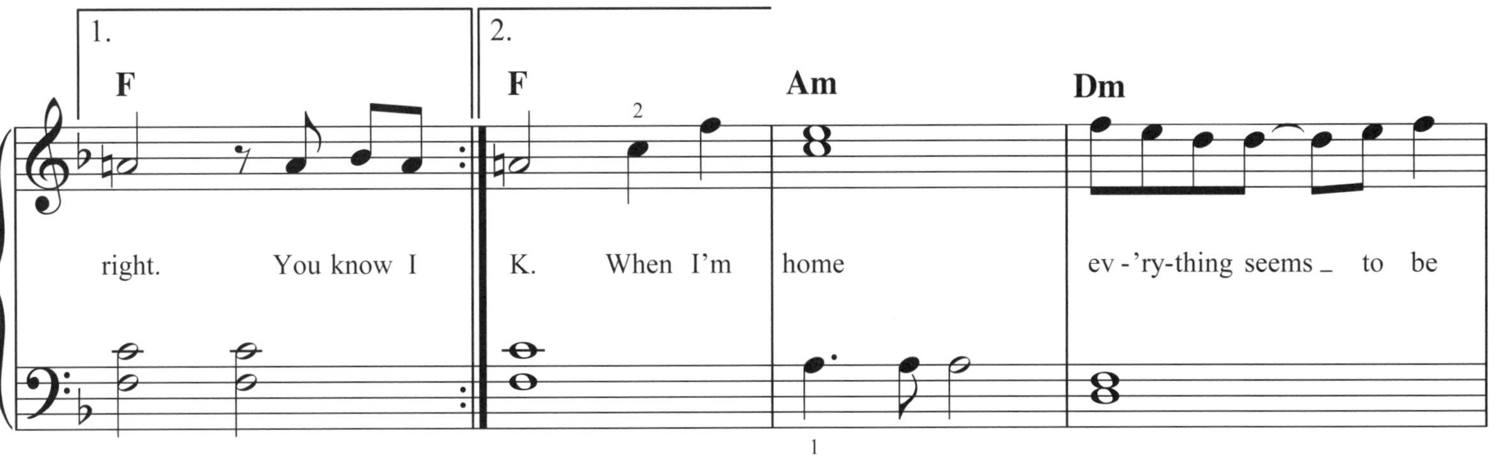
1.
2.
F
F
Am
Dm
right. You know I
K. When I'm
home
ev - 'ry-thing seems _ to be

Am
F
Dm
al - right,
when I'm
home
feel-ing you hold - ing me

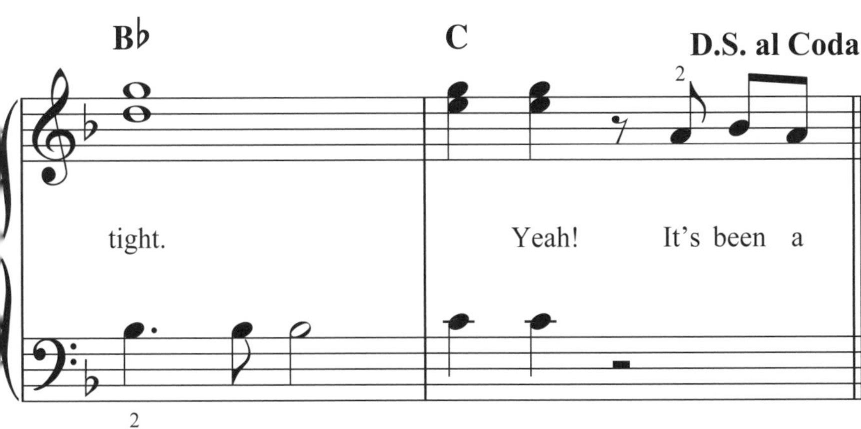
B♭
C
D.S. al Coda
tight.
Yeah! It's been a

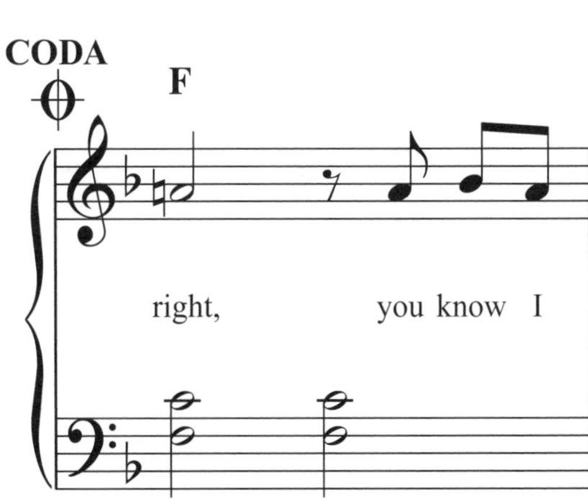
CODA
F
right, you know I

B♭7
F
B♭(add2)
F
feel _ al -
right, you know I
feel al -
right.

HELP!

Words and Music by JOHN LENNON
and PAUL McCARTNEY

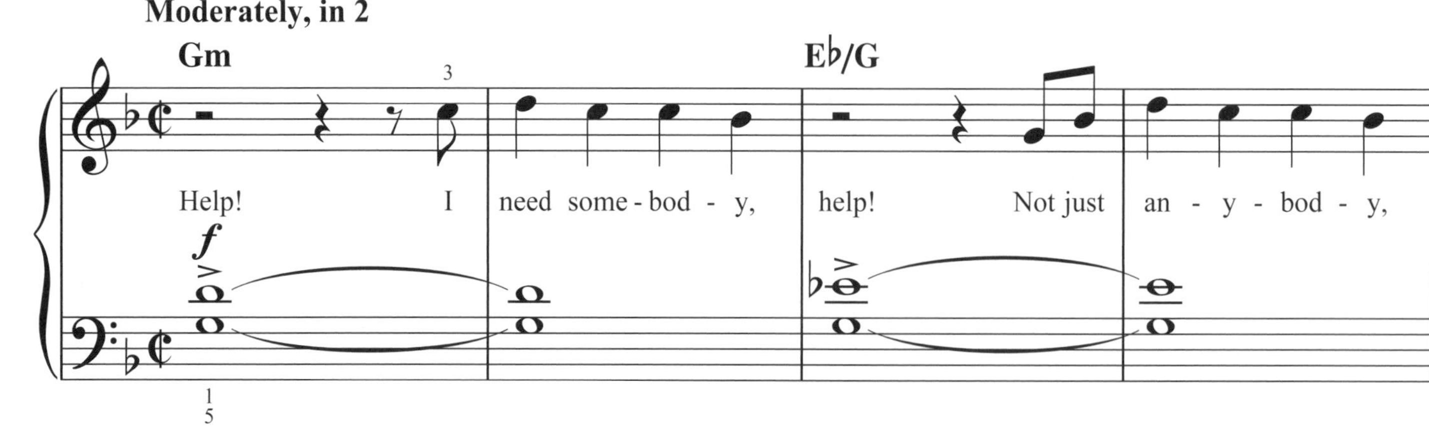

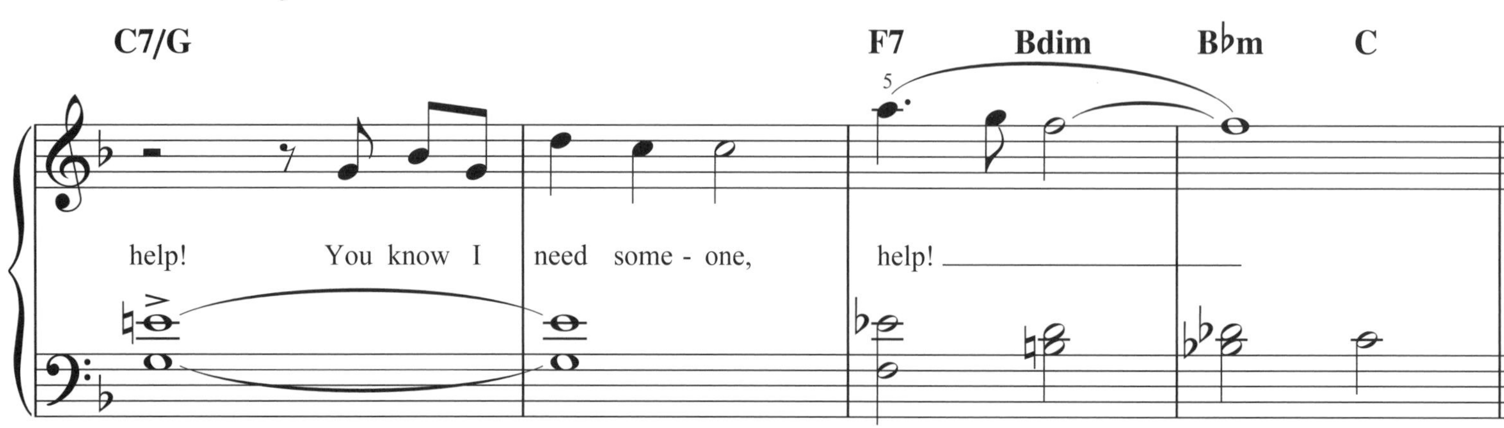

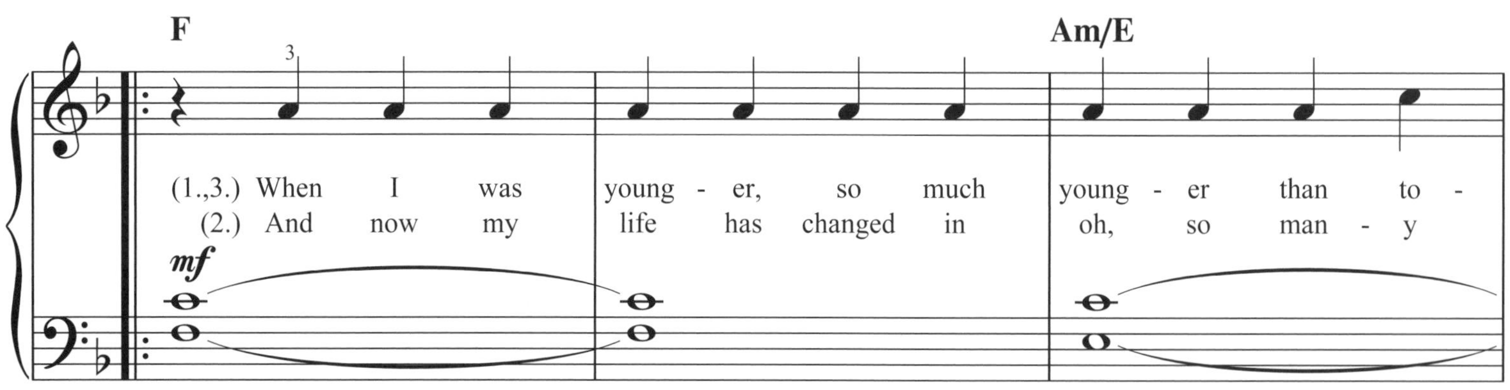

B♭
E♭
F
help in an - y way.
van - ish in the haze.
But now these days are gone, I'm
But ev - 'ry now and then I

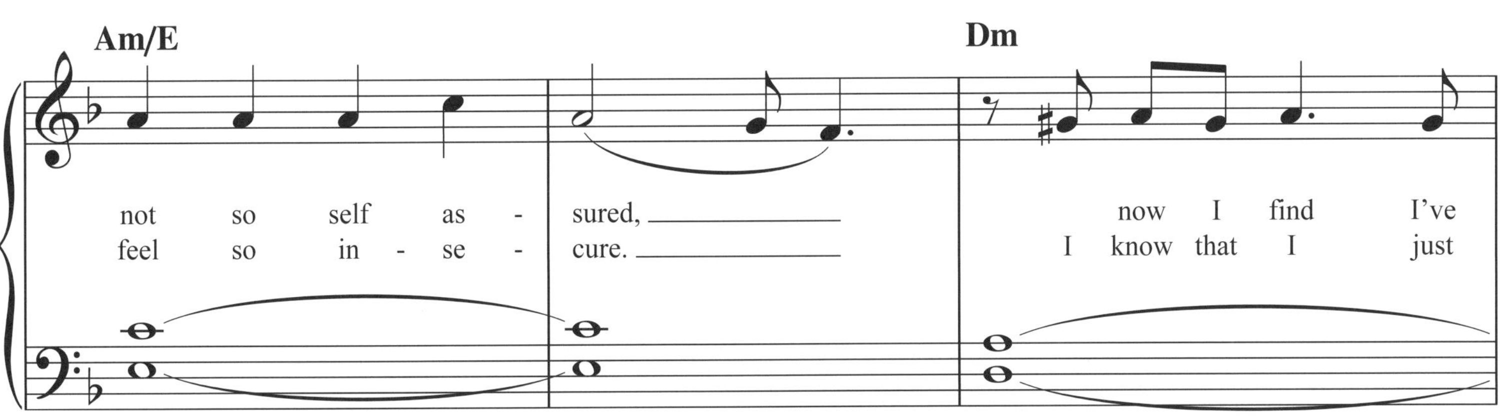
Am/E
Dm
not so self as - sured,
feel so in - se - cure.
now I find I've
I know that I just

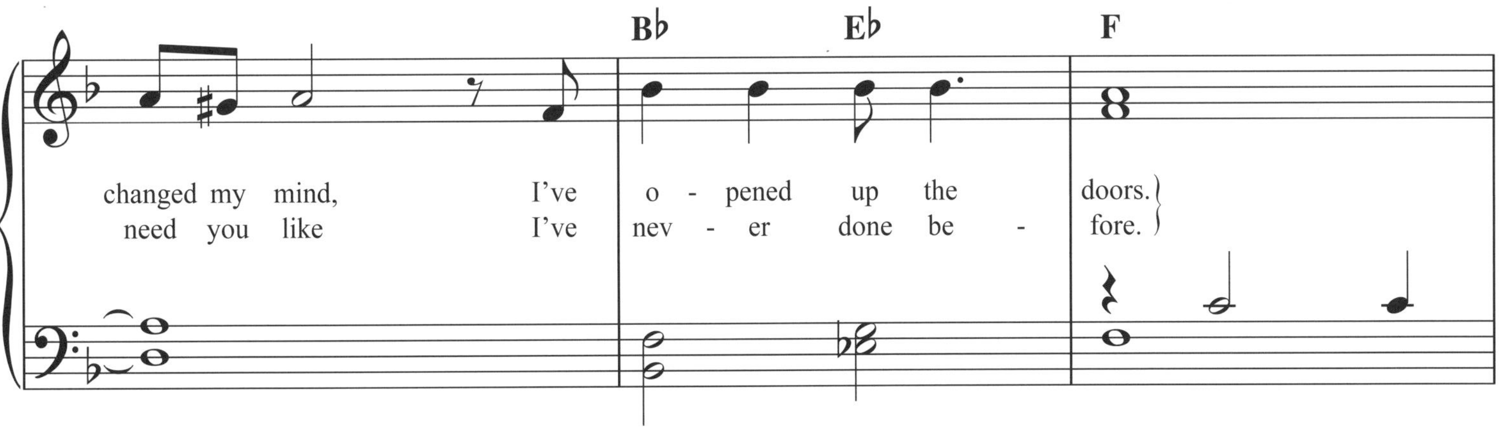
B♭
E♭
F
changed my mind, I've o - pened up the doors.
need you like I've nev - er done be - fore.

Gm
Help me if you can, I'm feel - ing down, and I

E♭
do ap - pre - ci - ate you be - ing 'round.
3

C7
Help me get my feet back on the ground; won't you
1

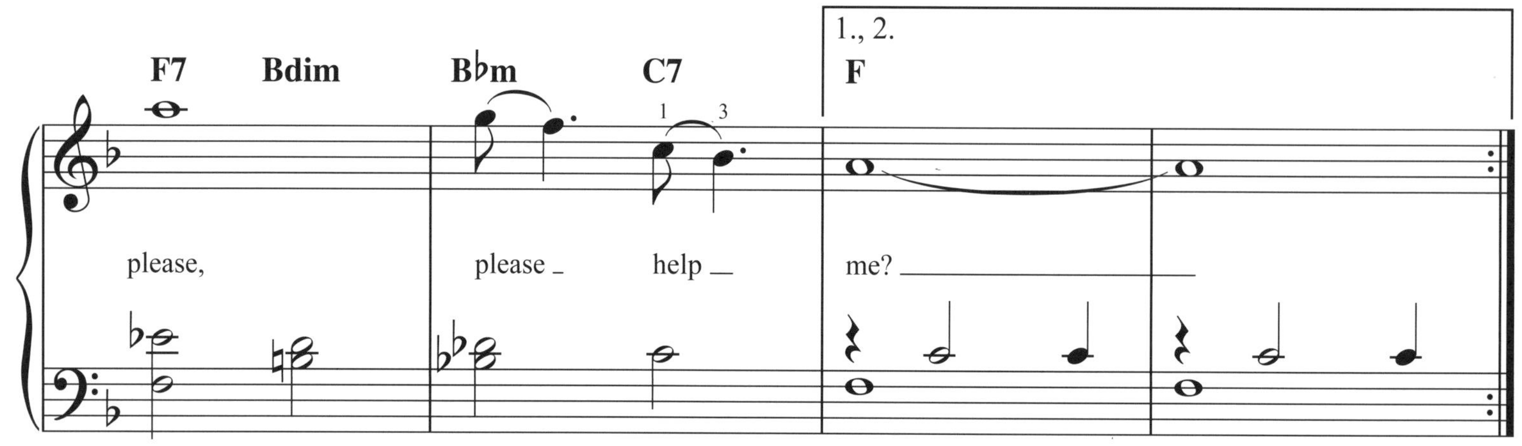
F7 Bdim B♭m C7
1., 2.
F
please, please help me?
1 3

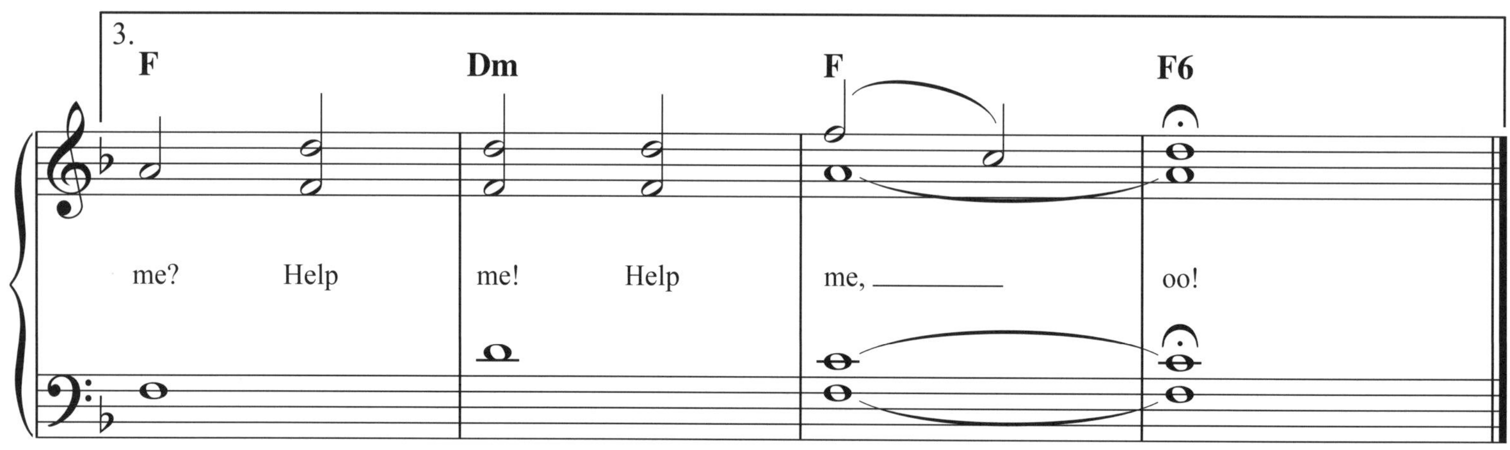
3.
F Dm F F6
me? Help me! Help me, oo!

HERE COMES THE SUN

Words and Music by
GEORGE HARRISON

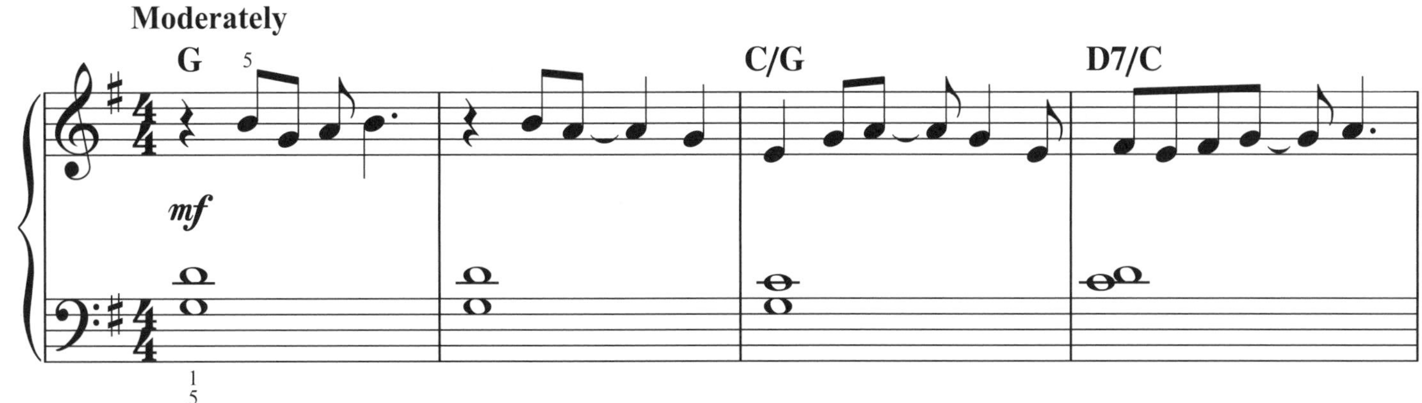

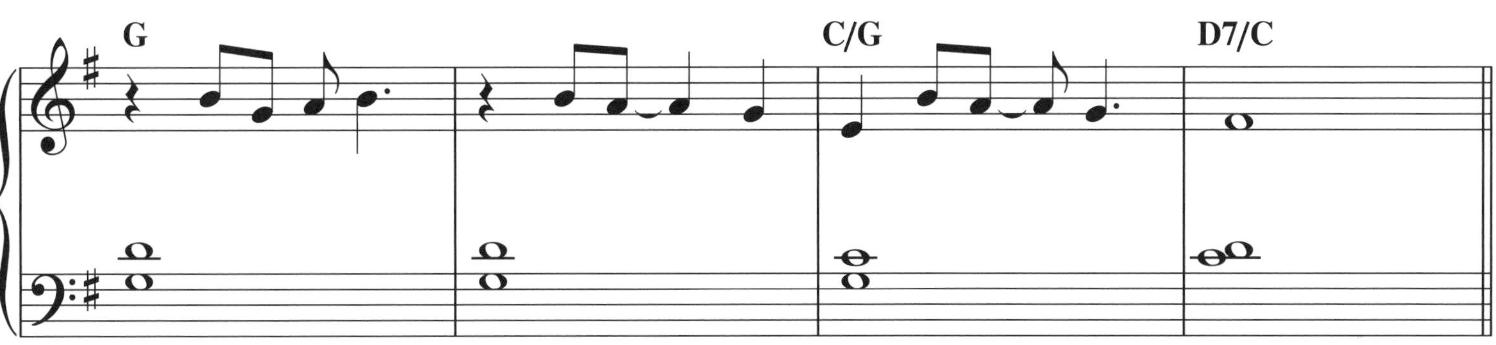

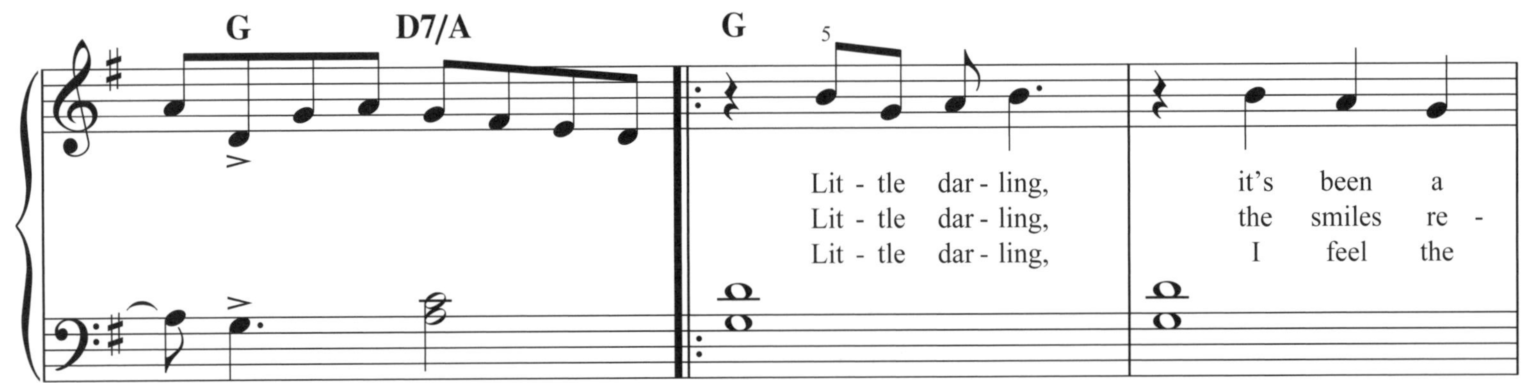
G
D7/A
G
Lit - tle dar - ling, it's been a
Lit - tle dar - ling, the smiles re -
Lit - tle dar - ling, I feel the

C/G
D7/F♯
G
long, cold, lone - ly win - ter. Lit - tle dar - ling,
turn - ing to their fac - es. Lit - tle dar - ling,
ice is slow - ly melt - ing. Lit - tle dar - ling,

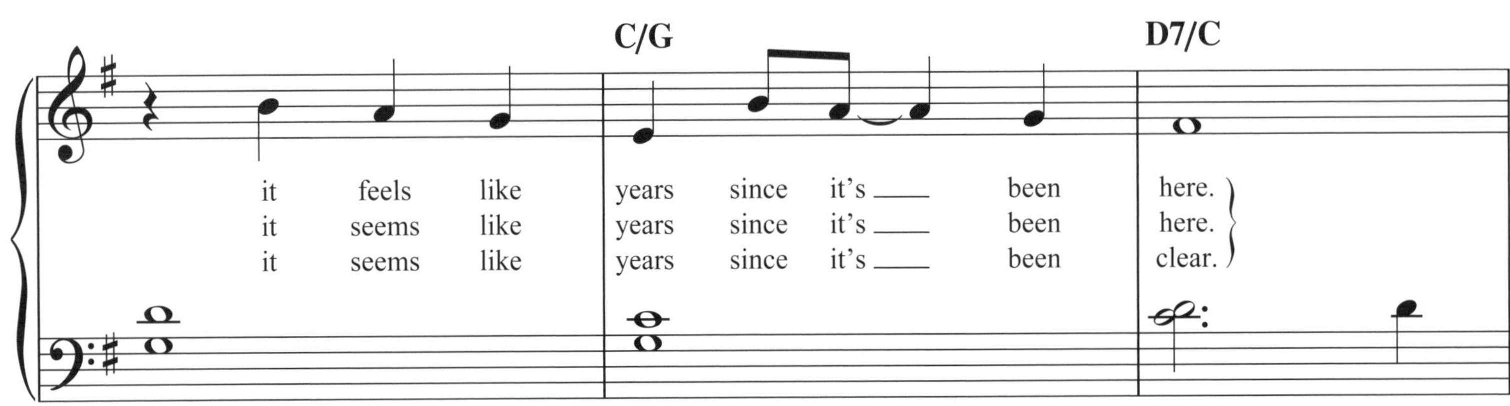
C/G
D7/C
it feels like years since it's been here.
it seems like years since it's been here.
it seems like years since it's been clear.

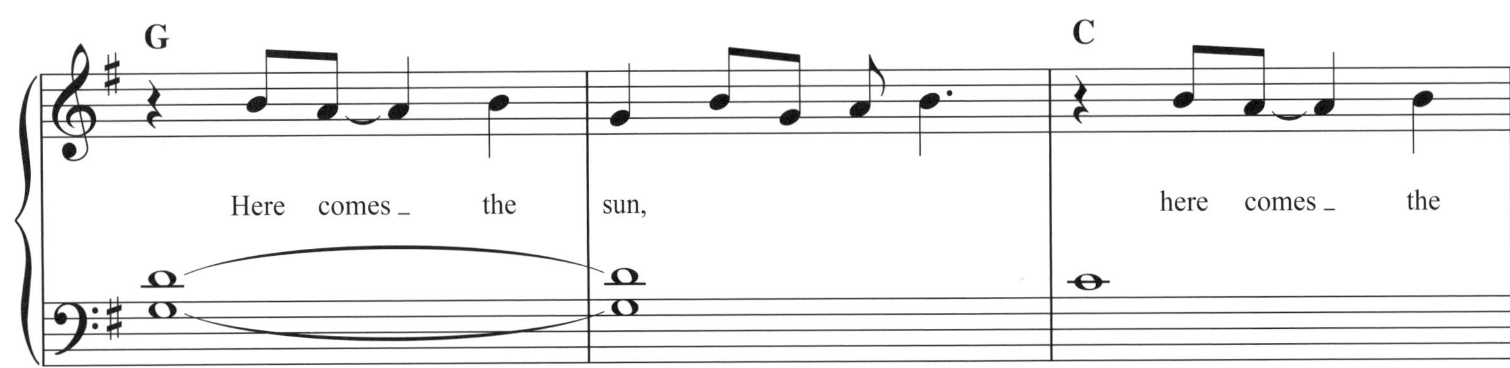
G
C
Here comes the sun, here comes the

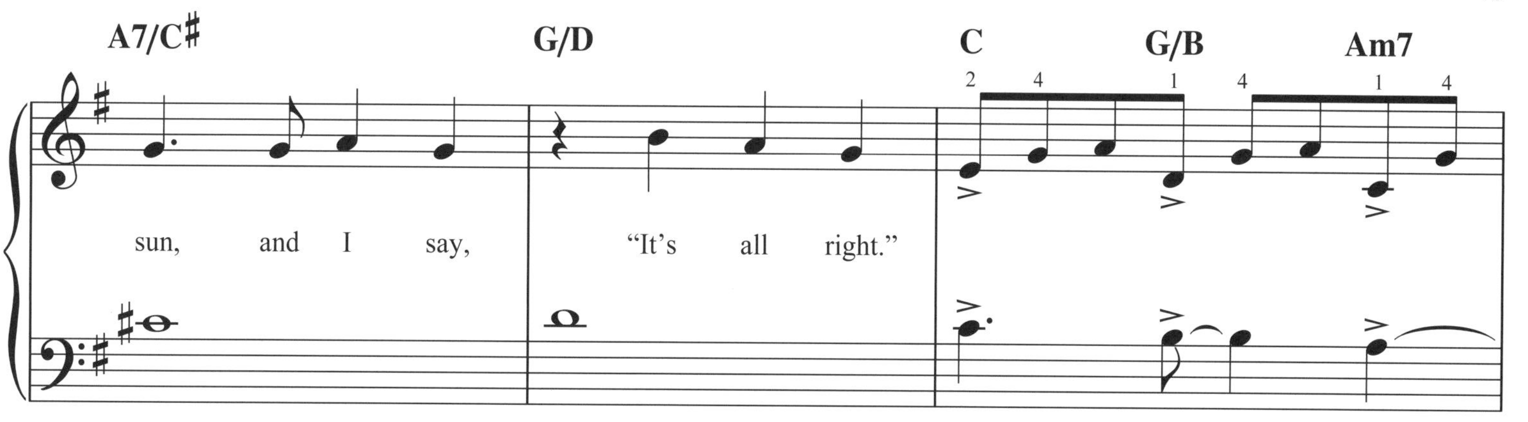
A7/C♯
G/D
C
G/B
Am7
2 4 1 4 1 4
sun, and I say,
"It's all right."

1., 2.
G
D7/A
G
D7/C

3.
G
D7/A
G
C
G/B
Am7
"It's all right."

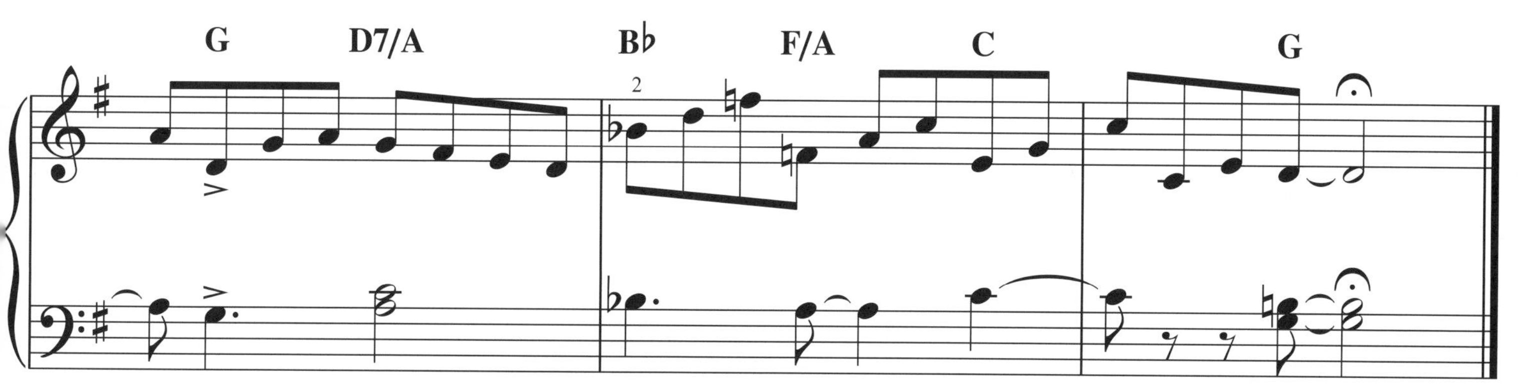
G
D7/A
B♭
F/A
C
G
2

HEY JUDE

Words and Music by JOHN LENNON
and PAUL McCARTNEY

Slowly and steadily

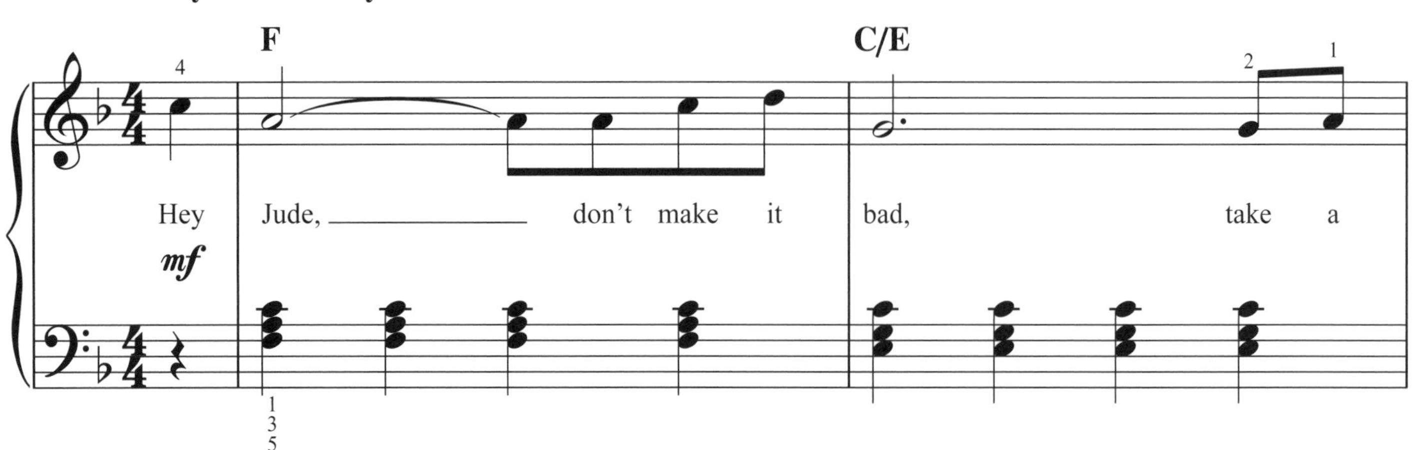

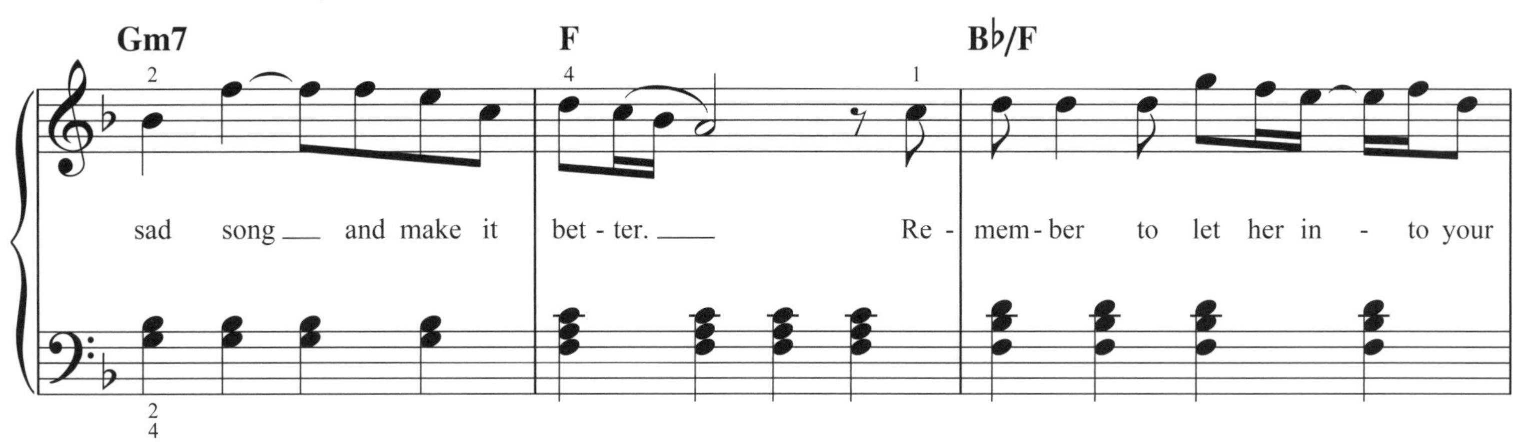

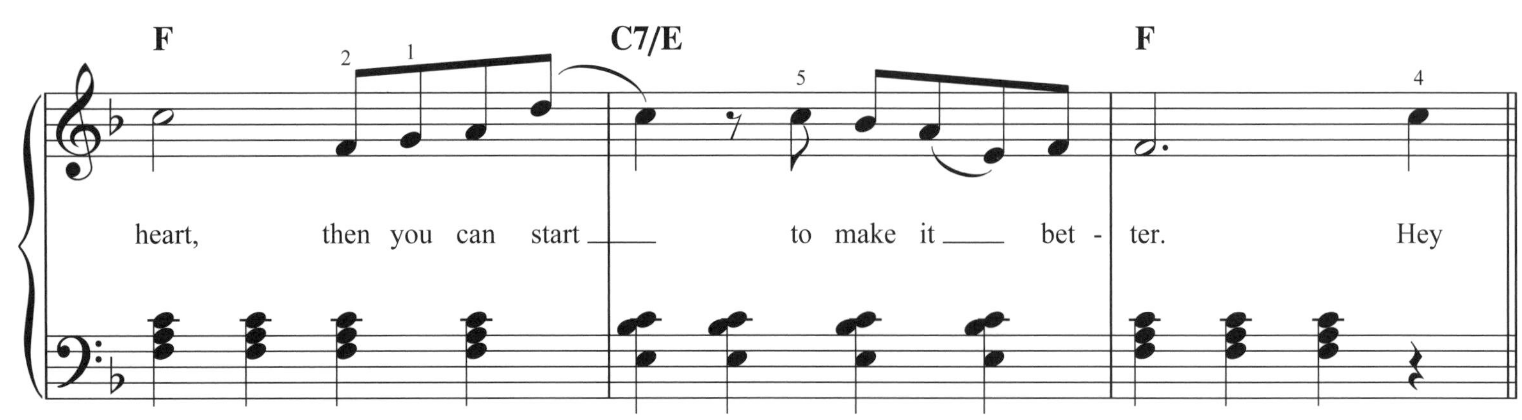

F
C/E
Gm7
Jude, don't be a - fraid; you were made to go out and
Jude, don't let me down; you have found her, now go and

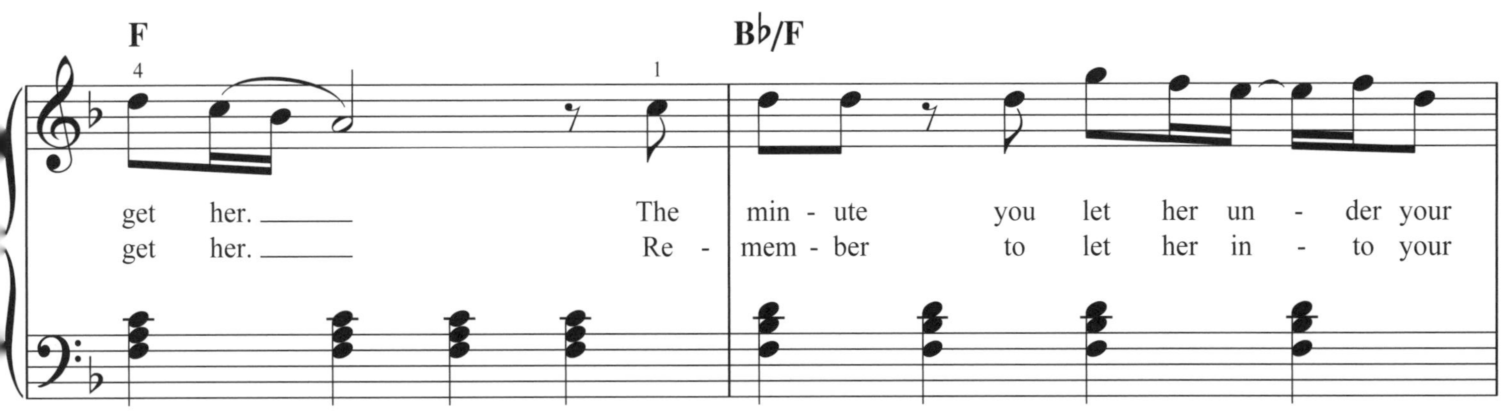
F
B♭/F
4
1
get her. The min - ute you let her un - der your
get her. Re - mem - ber to let her in - to your

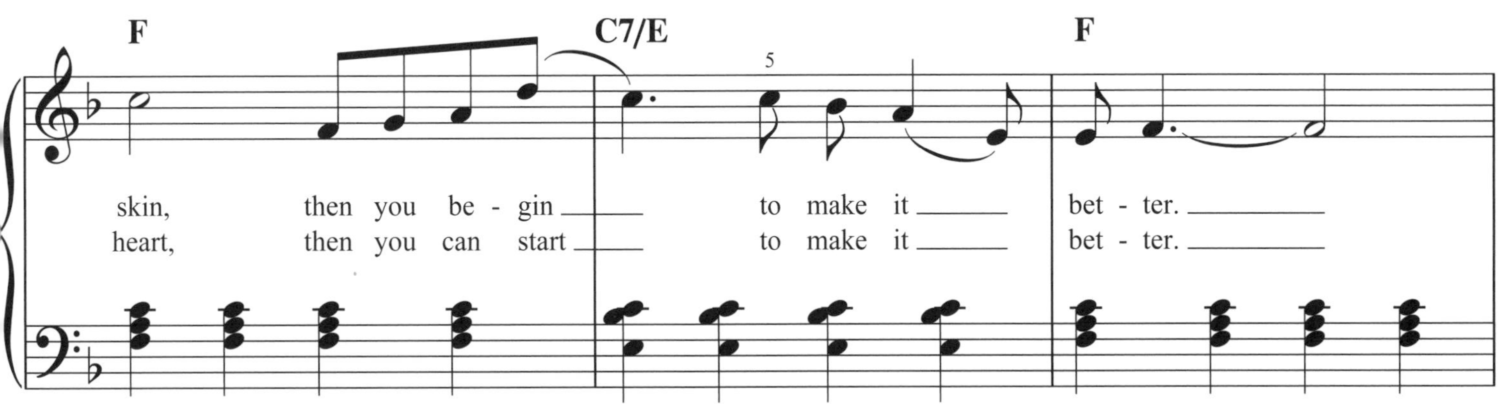
F
C7/E
F
5
skin, then you be - gin to make it bet - ter.
heart, then you can start to make it bet - ter.

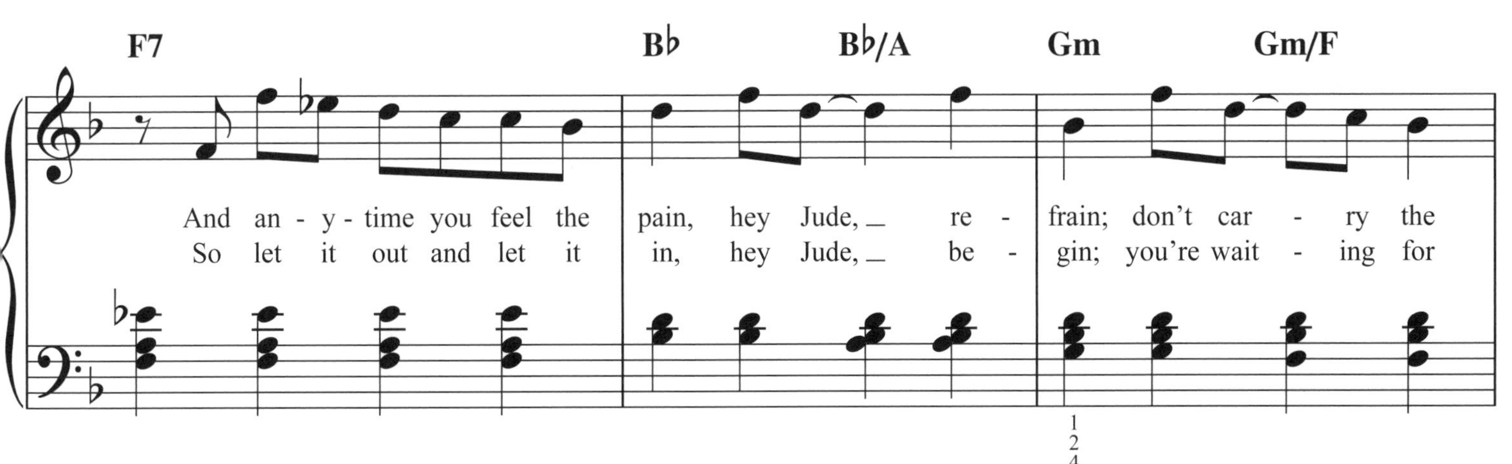
F7
B♭
B♭/A
Gm
Gm/F
And an - y - time you feel the pain, hey Jude, re - frain; don't car - ry the
So let it out and let it in, hey Jude, be - gin; you're wait - ing for
1
2
4

C7/E
F
F7
world up - on ___ your shoul - ders. ___
some - one to ___ per - form with. ___
For well you know that it's a
And don't you know that it's just

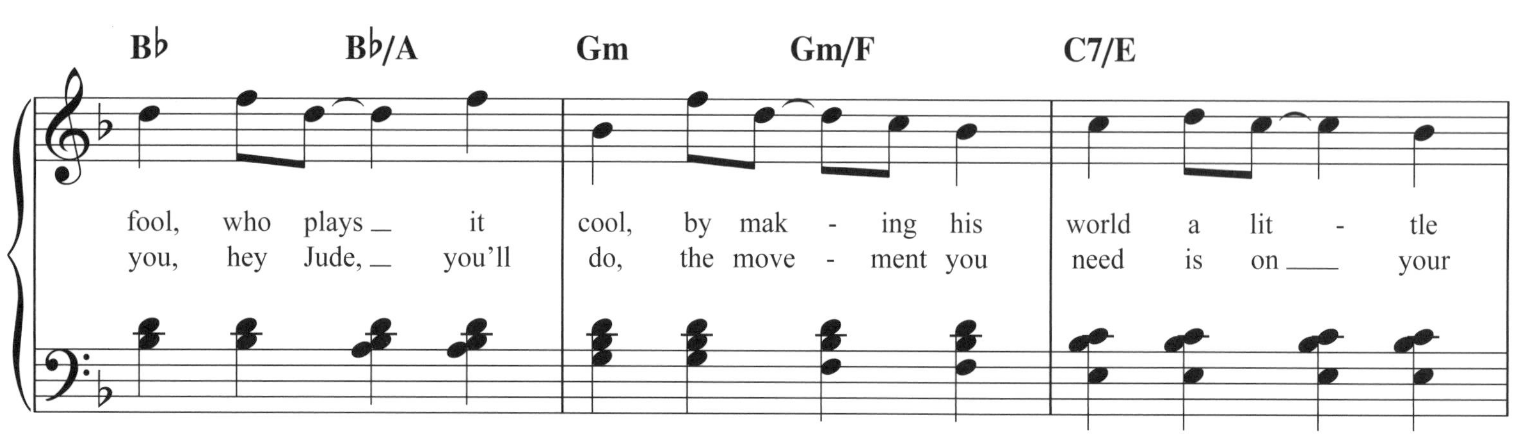
B♭
B♭/A
Gm
Gm/F
C7/E
fool, who plays ___ it cool, by mak - ing his world a lit - tle
you, hey Jude, ___ you'll do, the move - ment you need is on ___ your

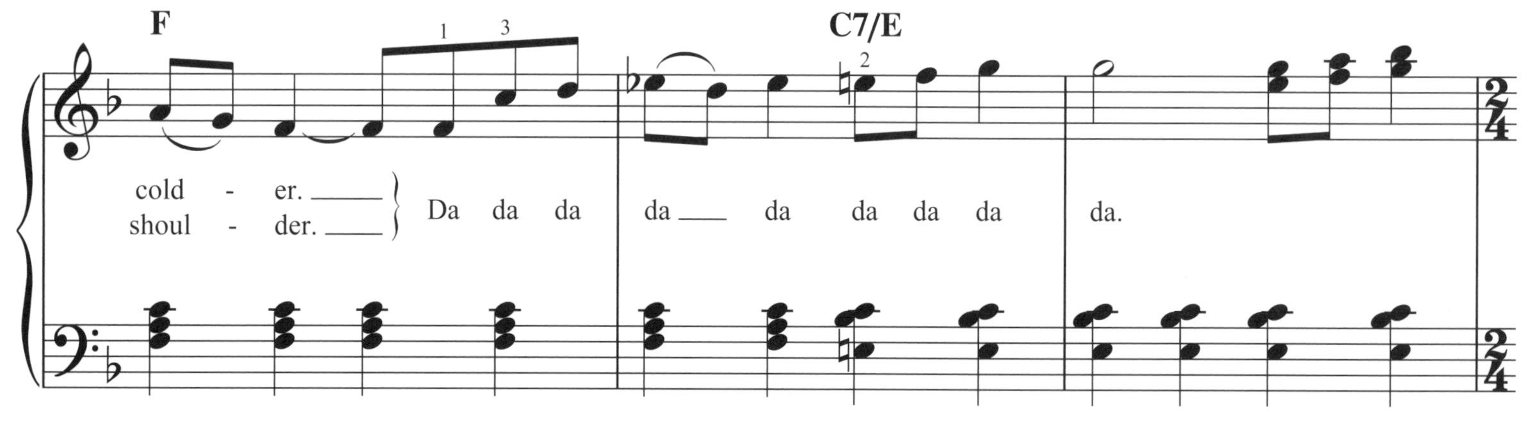
F
C7/E
cold - er. ___
shoul - der. ___
Da da da da ___ da da da da da.

1.
2.
F
Hey
Hey
Jude, ___ don't make it

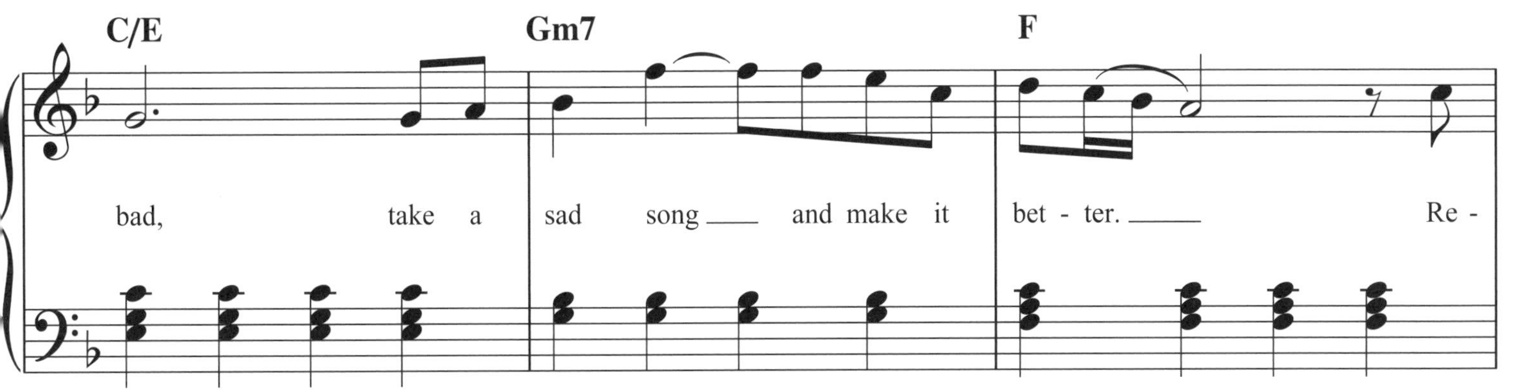
C/E
Gm7
F
bad, take a sad song ___ and make it bet - ter. ___ Re -

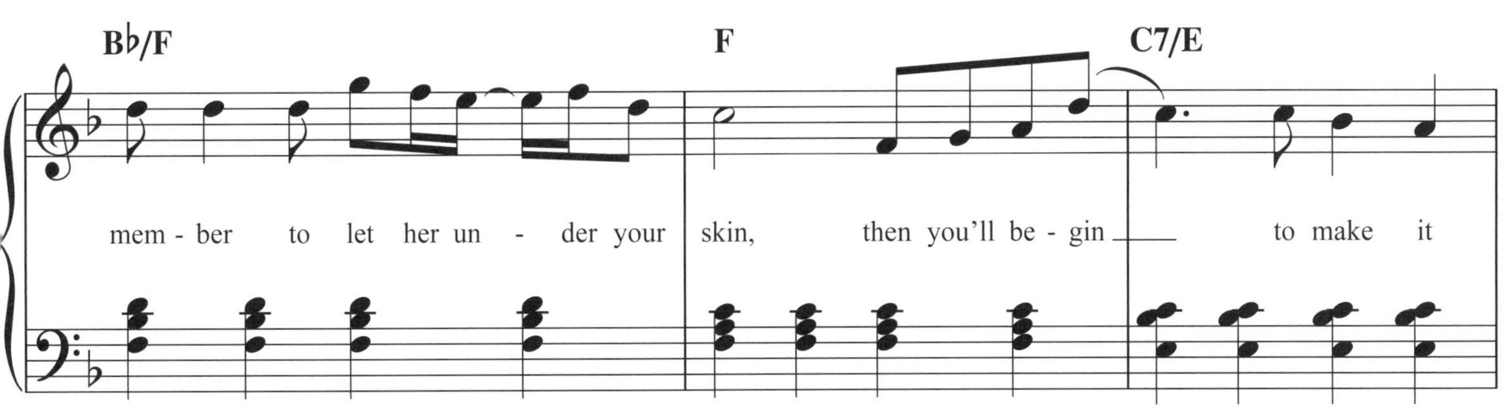
B♭/F
F
C7/E
mem - ber to let her un - der your skin, then you'll be - gin ___ to make it

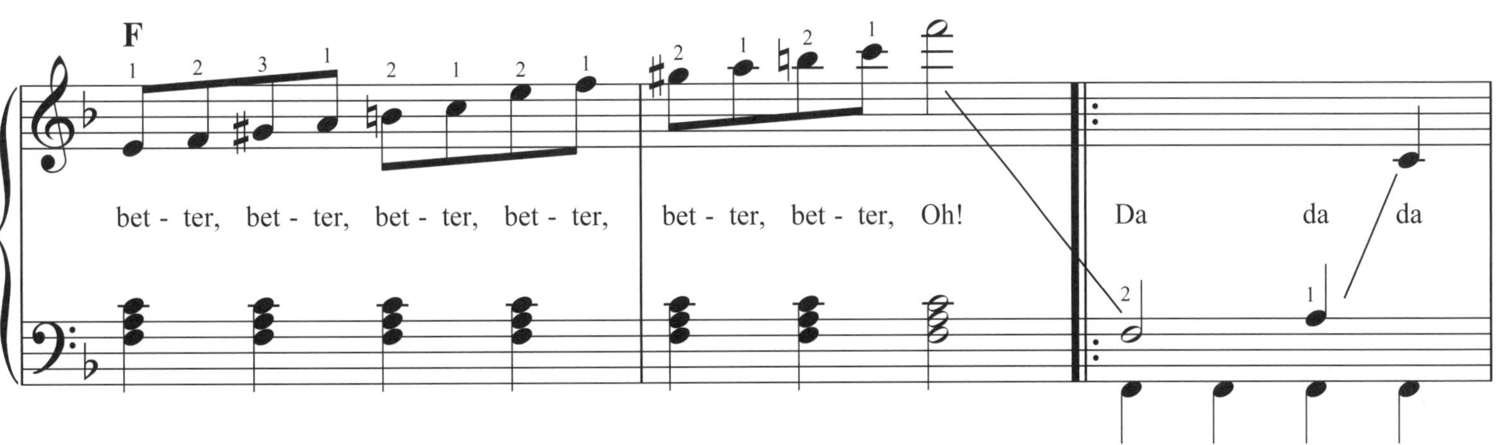
F
bet - ter, bet - ter, bet - ter, bet - ter, bet - ter, bet - ter, Oh! Da da da

Repeat and Fade
Optional Ending
E♭
B♭
F
da da da da da da da da, hey _ Jude.

I SAW HER STANDING THERE

Words and Music by JOHN LENNON
and PAUL McCARTNEY

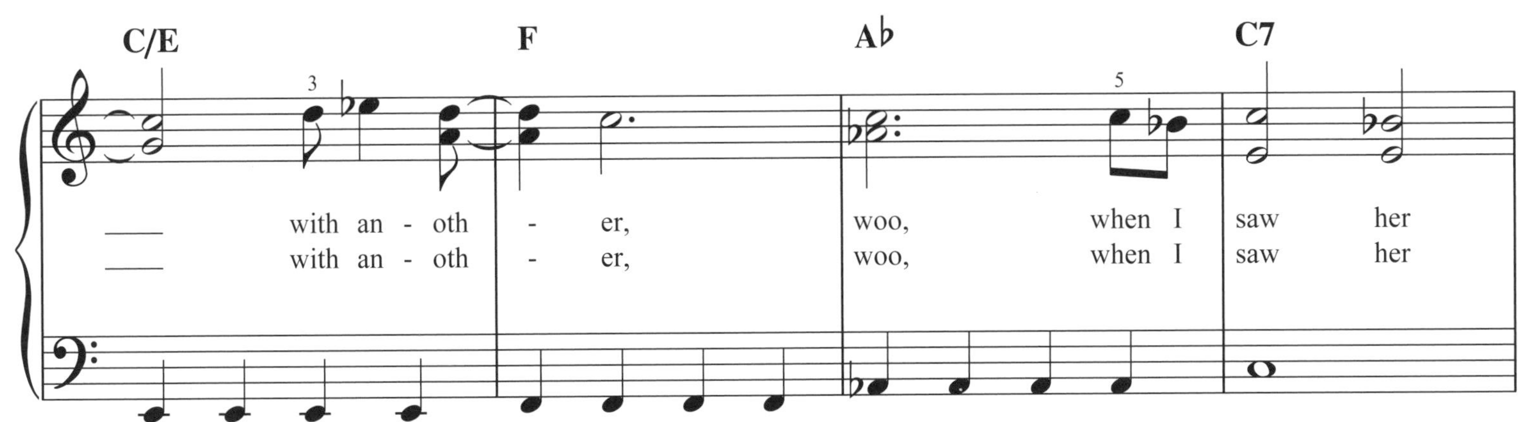
C/E
F
A♭
C7
with an - oth - er,
woo, when I saw her
with an - oth - er,
woo, when I saw her

G7
C7
1.
2.
stand - ing there?
Well, she
stand - ing there.
Well, my

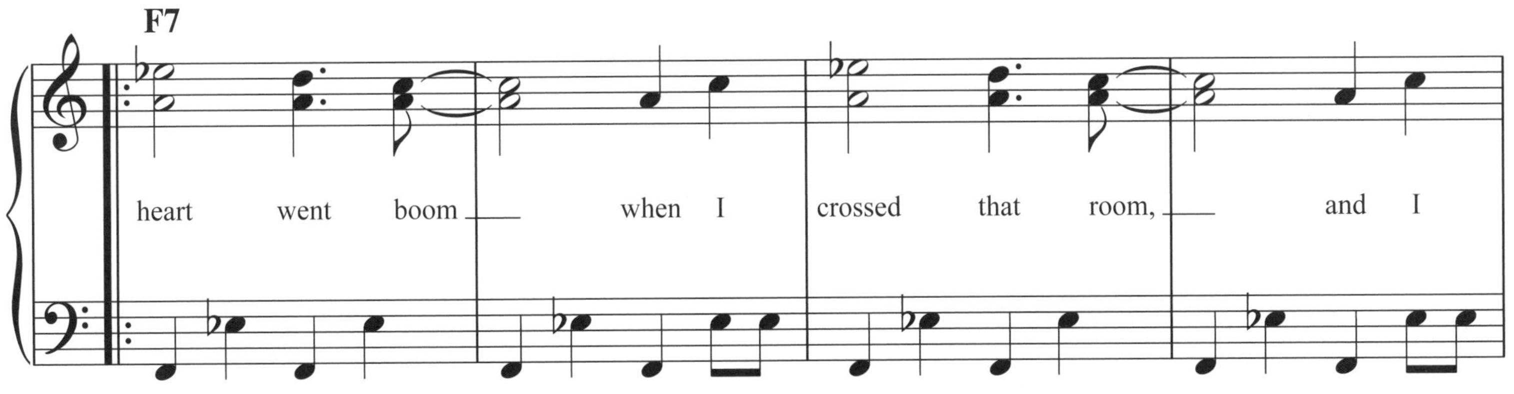
F7
heart went boom when I crossed that room, and I

G
held her hand in mine,

F7
C7
4
mine. Oh, we danced through the night

F7
C7
and we held each oth - er tight, and be -

G7
fore too long I fell in love with her. Now

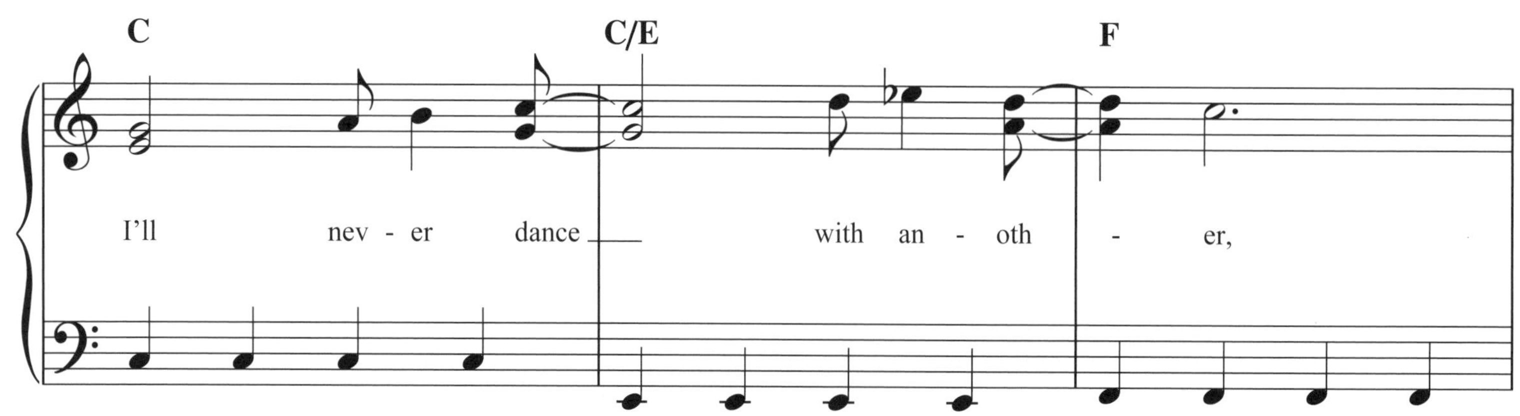
C
C/E
F
I'll nev - er dance with an - oth - er,

1.
A♭
C7
G7
C7
oh, since I saw her stand - ing there.

2.
C7
Well, my there. Oh, since I

G7
C7
saw her stand - ing there. Yeah, well, since I

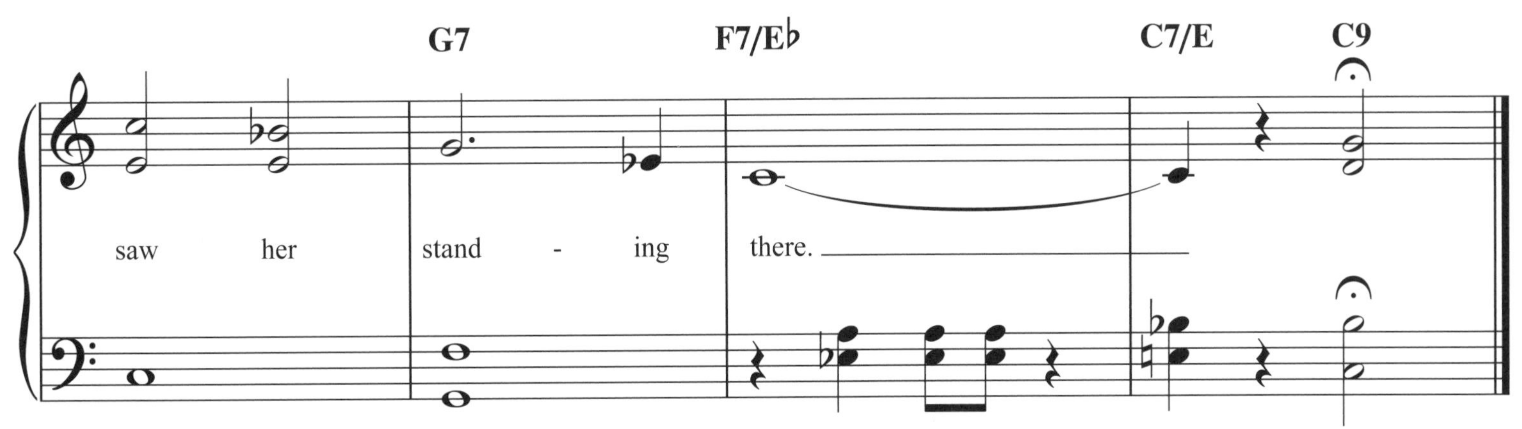
G7
F7/E♭
C7/E
C9
saw her stand - ing there.

SOMETHING

Words and Music by
GEORGE HARRISON

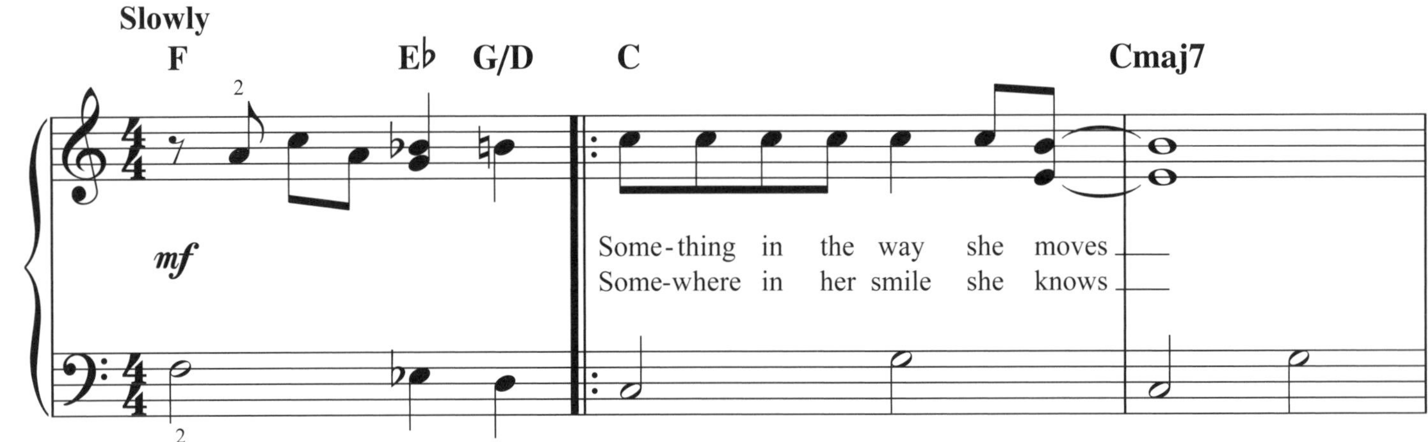

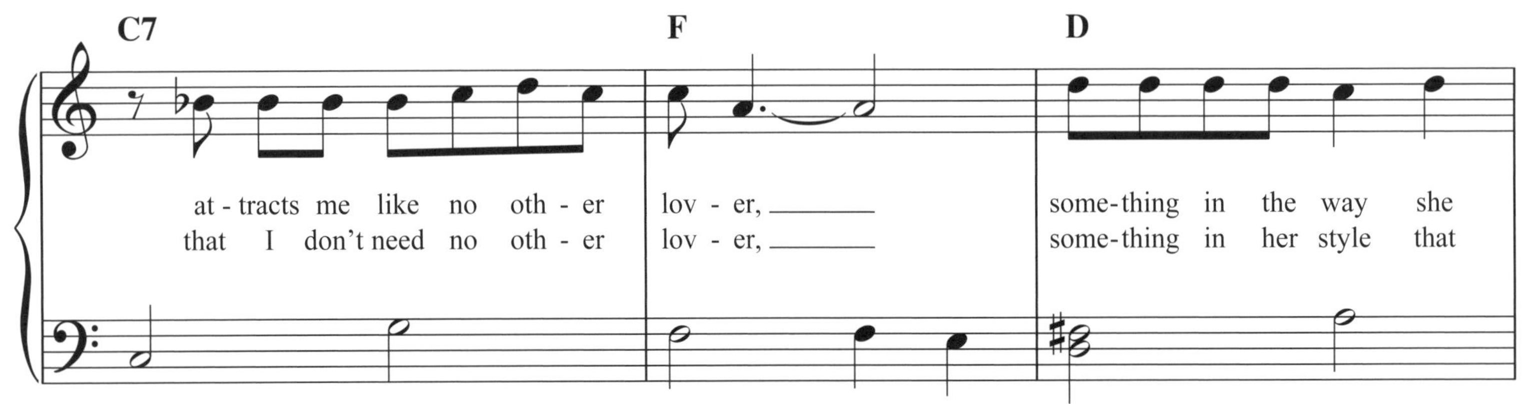

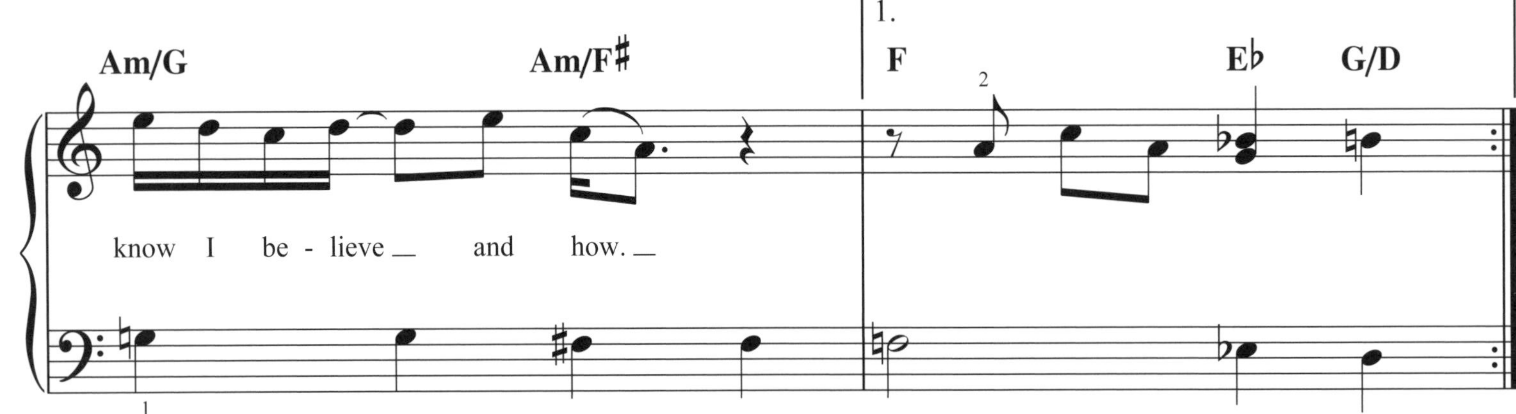

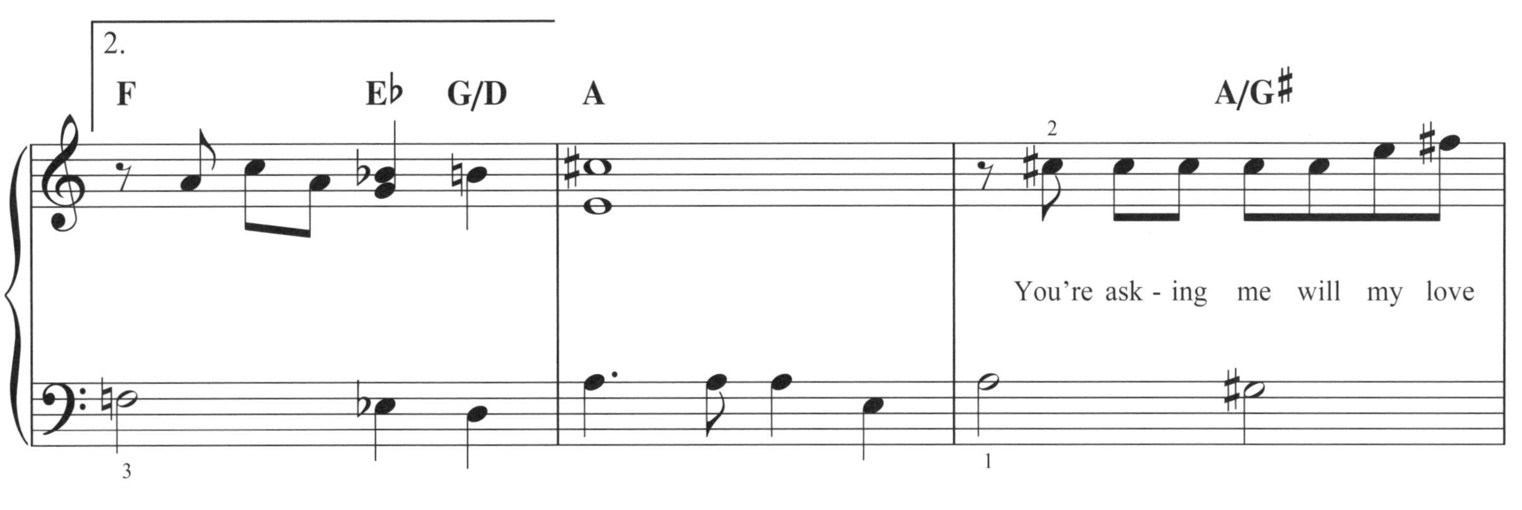
2.
F Eb G/D A A/G#
You're ask - ing me will my love

F#m F#m/E D G A
grow? I don't know, I don't know.

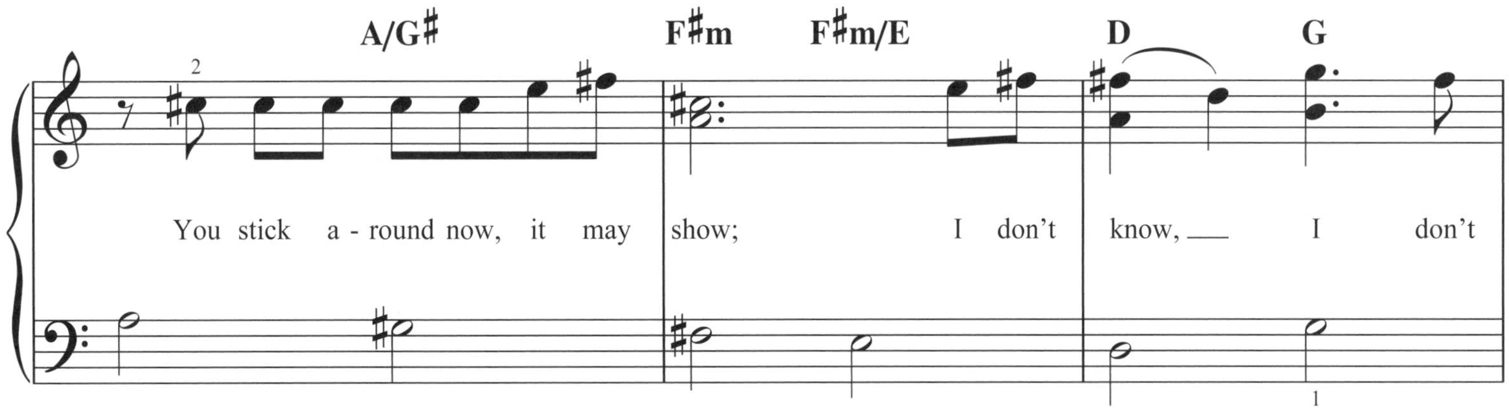
A/G# F#m F#m/E D G
You stick a - round now, it may show; I don't know, I don't

C Cmaj7
know. Some-thing in the way she knows,

C7
F
D7
and all I have to do is think of her, some-thing in the things she

G
Am
Am/G♯
shows __ me. I don't want to leave __ her now, you

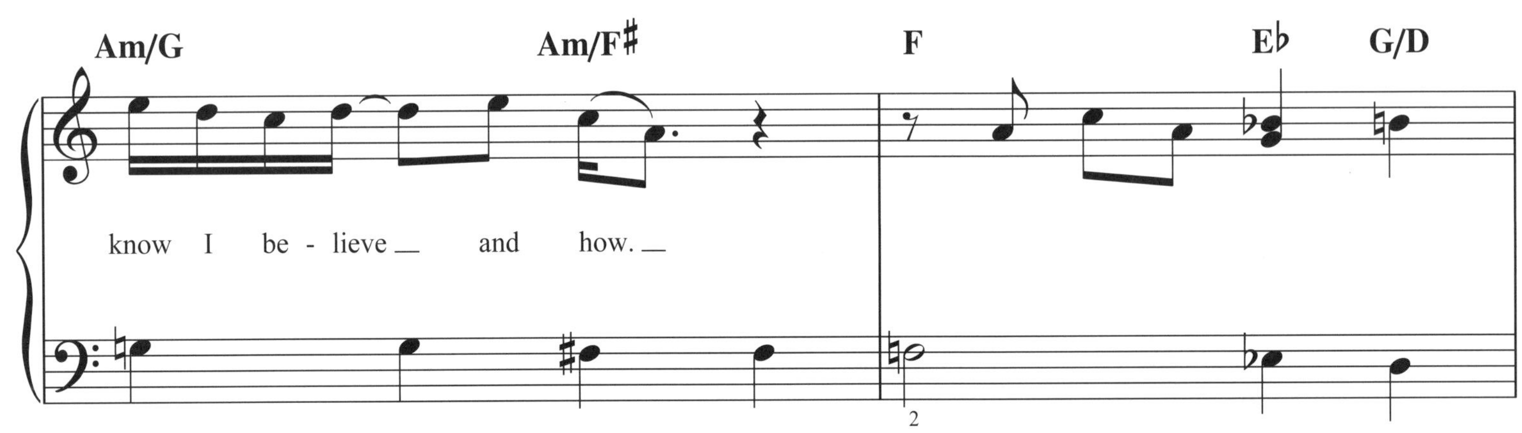
Am/G
Am/F♯
F
E♭
G/D
know I be - lieve __ and how. __
2

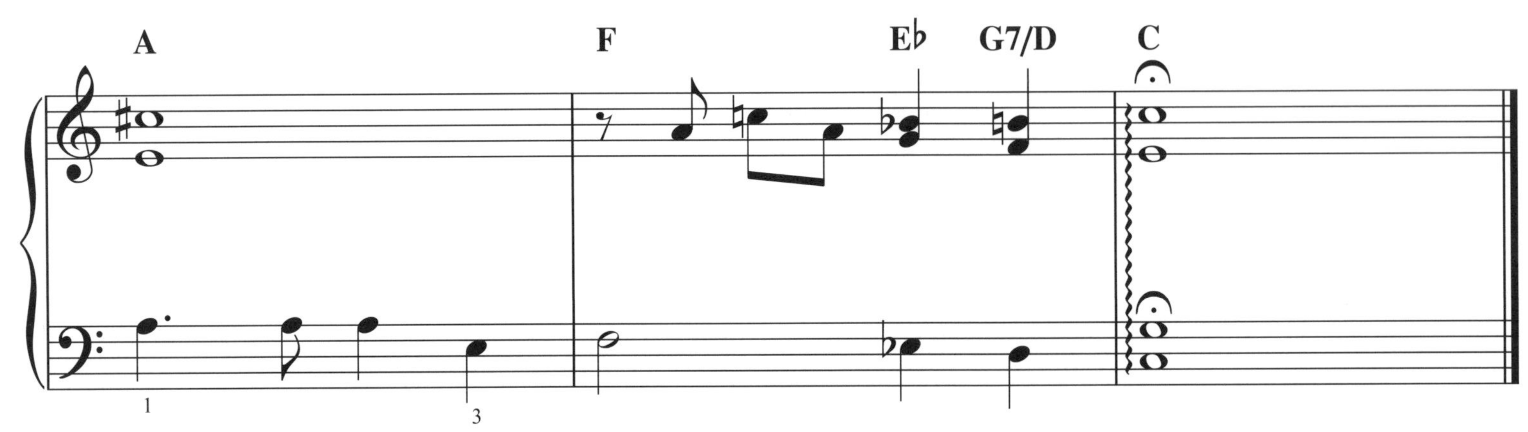
A
F
E♭
G7/D
C
1
3

I WANT TO HOLD YOUR HAND

Words and Music by JOHN LENNON
and PAUL McCARTNEY

2.
G
Dm7
G7
C
hand. And when I touch you I feel hap - py in -

Am
Dm7
G7
C
side. It's such a feel - ing that my love I can't hide,

D
C
D
C
D
I can't hide, I can't hide! Yeah,

G
D
Em
you got that some - thing I think you'll un - der -

Bm
G
D
stand. When
I
say
feel
that
some - thing,

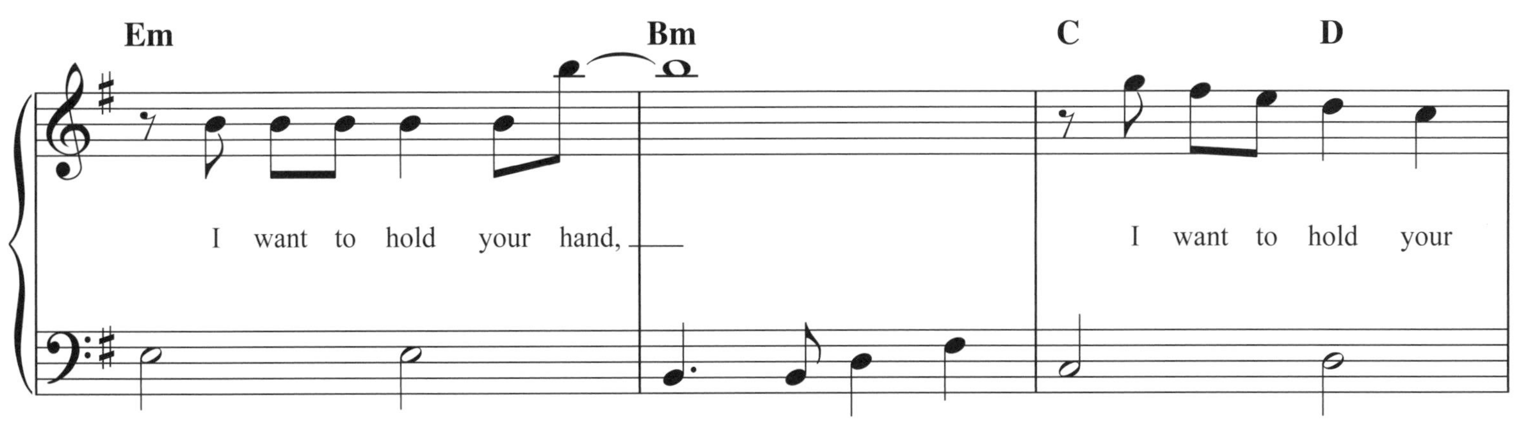
Em
Bm
C
D
I want to hold your hand,
I want to hold your

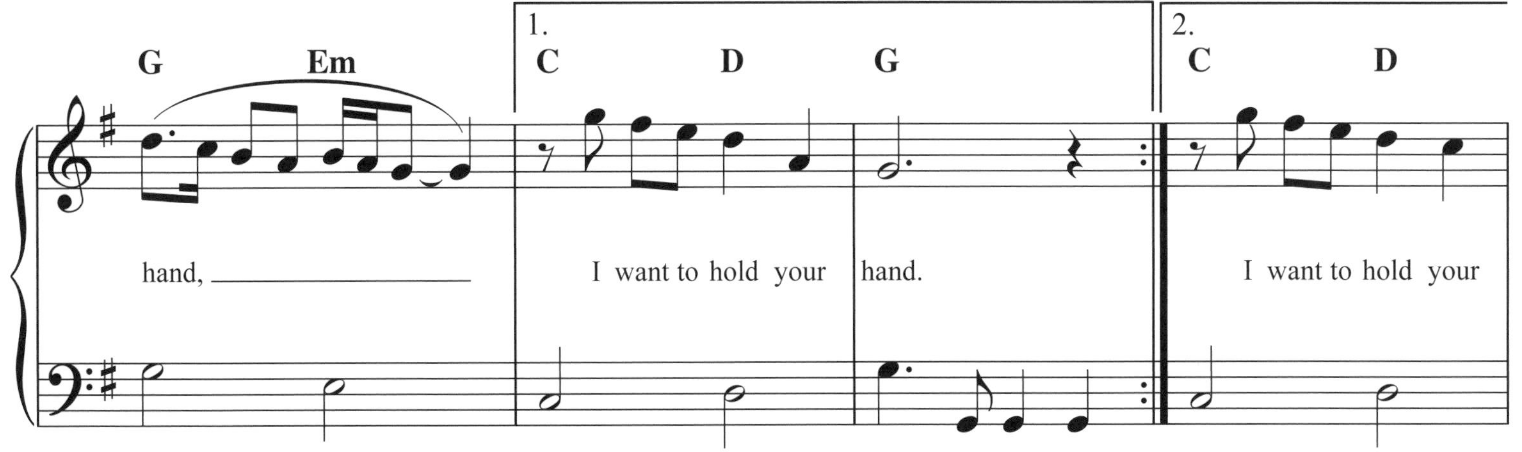
G
Em
1.
C
D
G
2.
C
D
hand,
I want to hold your
hand.
I want to hold your

B/D♯
C
D
C
G
hand,
I want to hold your
hand.

IN MY LIFE

Words and Music by JOHN LENNON
and PAUL McCARTNEY

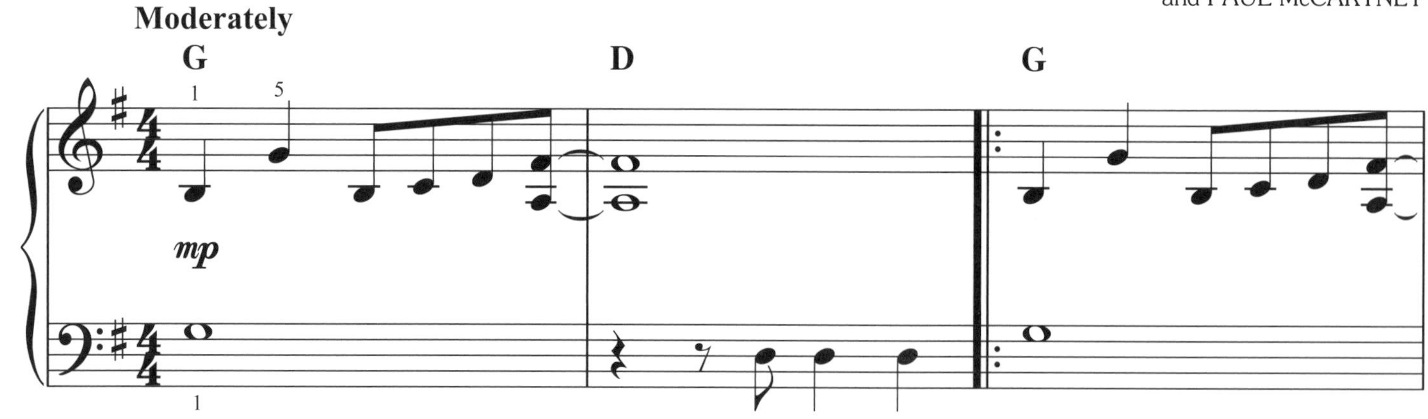

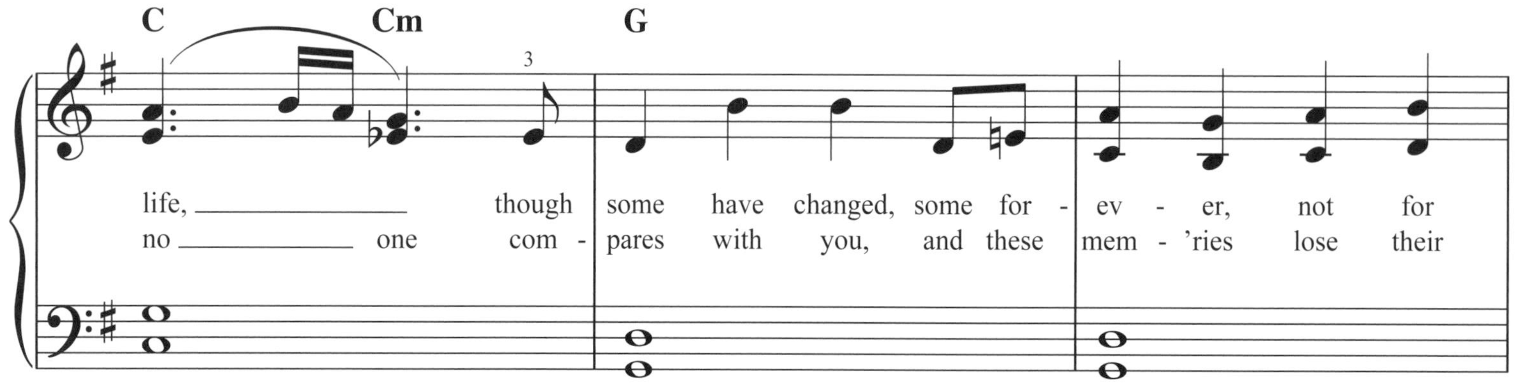

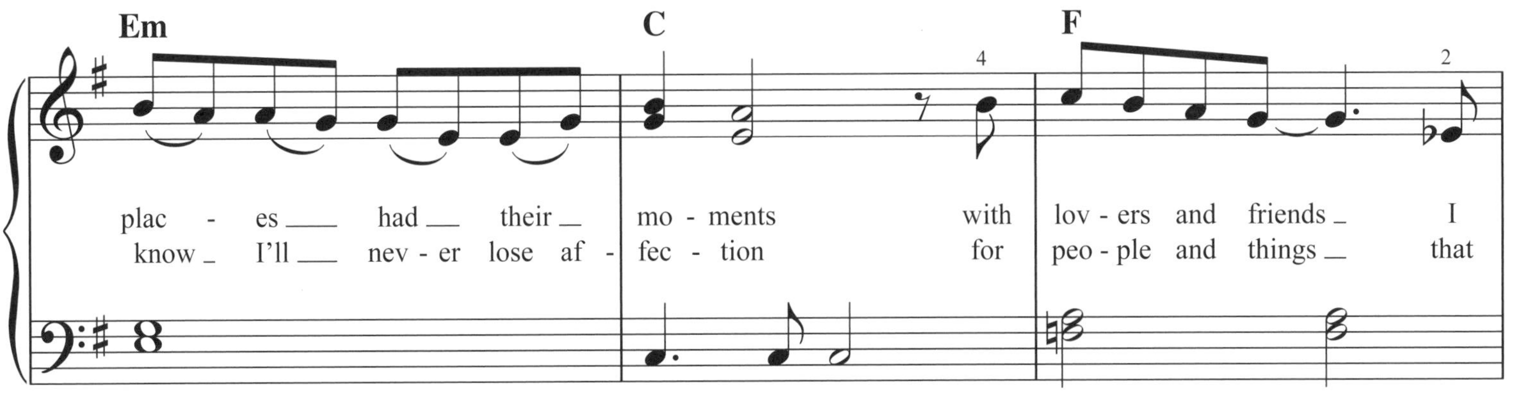
Em
C
F
places had their moments with lovers and friends I
know I'll never lose affection for people and things that

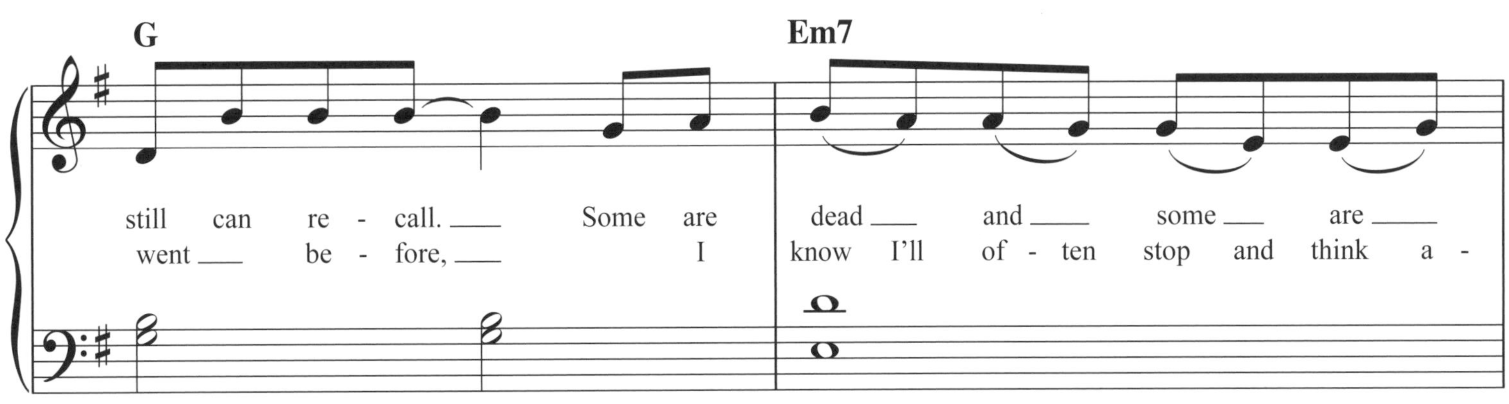
G
Em7
still can recall. Some are dead and some are
went before, I know I'll often stop and think a-

A7
Cm
G
living. In my life, I've loved them all.
bout them. In my life, I love you more.

D
D7
G
rit.

LET IT BE

Words and Music by JOHN LENNON
and PAUL McCARTNEY

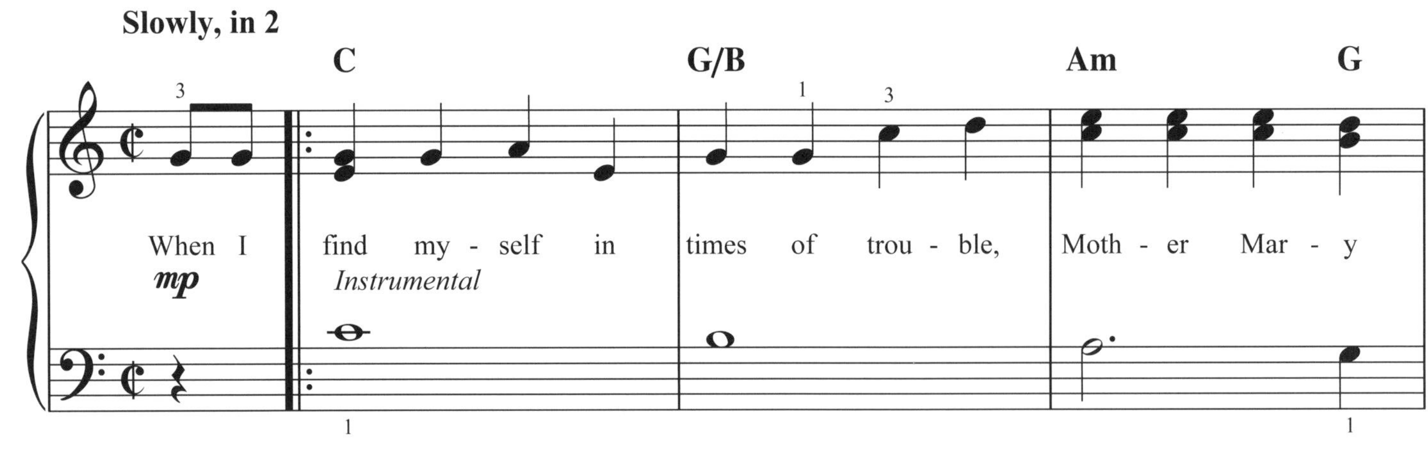

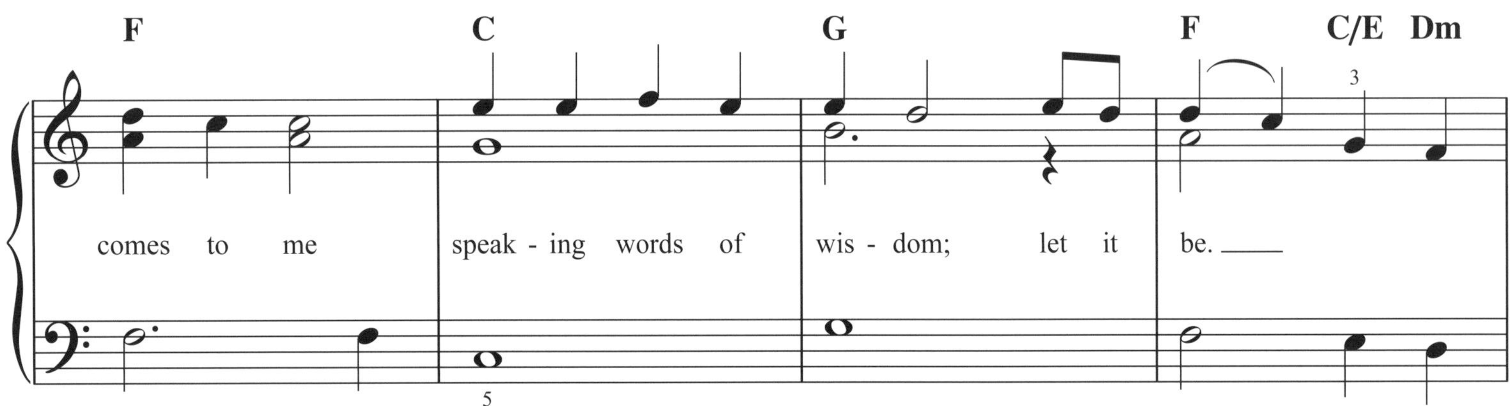

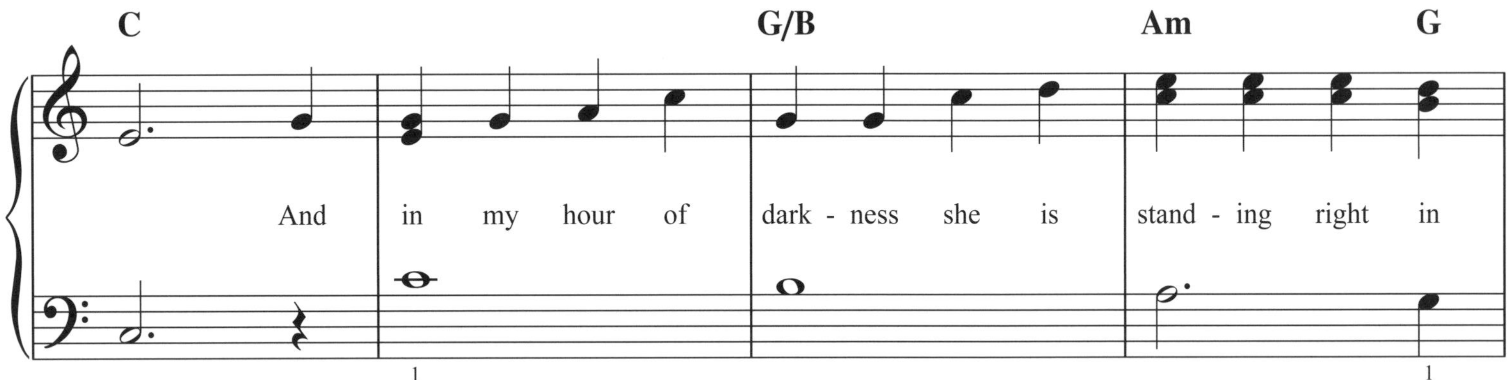

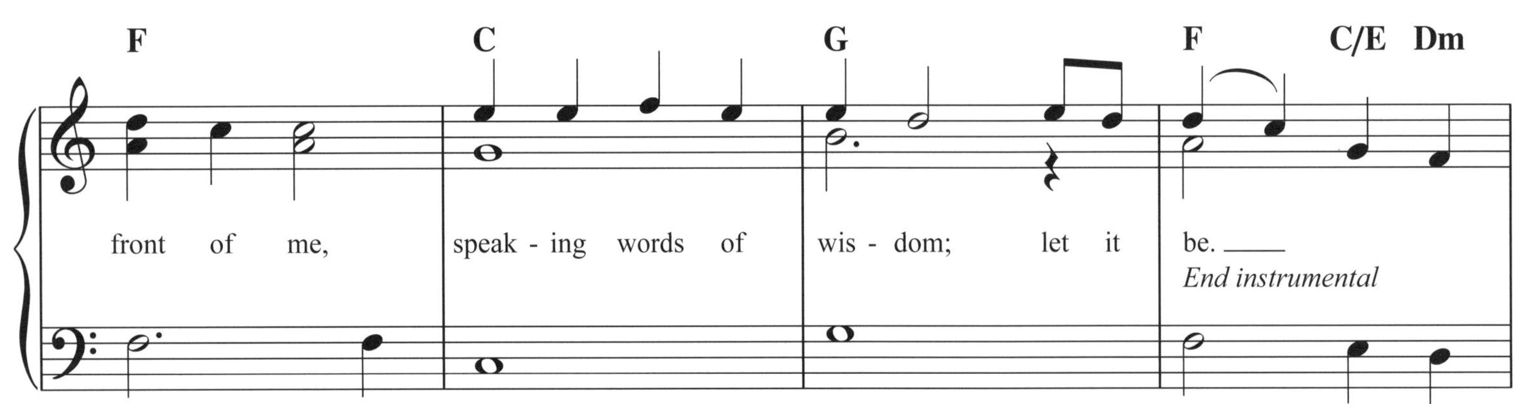

C Am G F
Let it be, let it be, let it be, let it
Let it be, let it be, let it be, let it

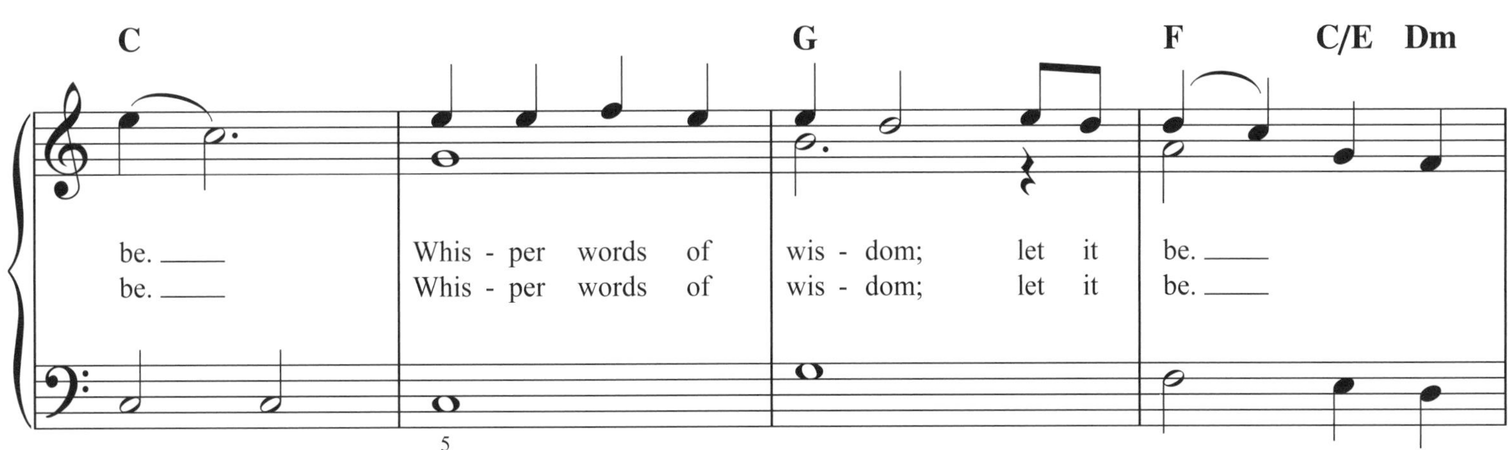
C G F C/E Dm
be. Whis - per words of wis - dom; let it be.
be. Whis - per words of wis - dom; let it be.

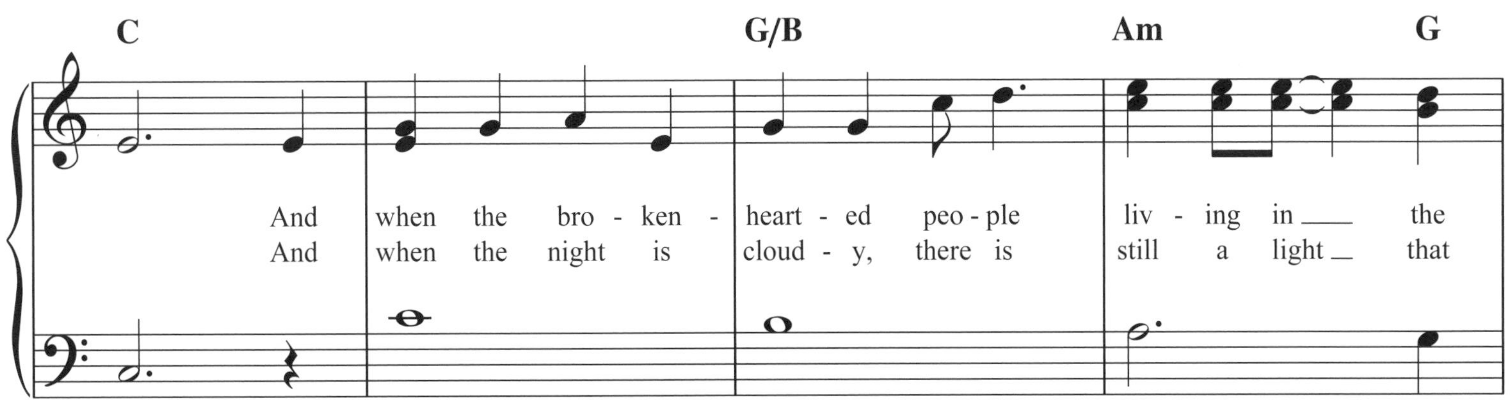
C G/B Am G
And when the bro - ken - heart - ed peo - ple liv - ing in the
And when the night is cloud - y, there is still a light that

F C G F C/E Dm
world a - gree, there will be an an - swer; let it be.
shines on me. Shine un - til to - mor - row; let it be.

C
G/B
For though they may be part - ed, there is
I wake up to the sound of mu - sic,

Am
G
F
C
still a chance that they will see, there will be an
Moth - er Mar - y comes to me, speak - ing words of

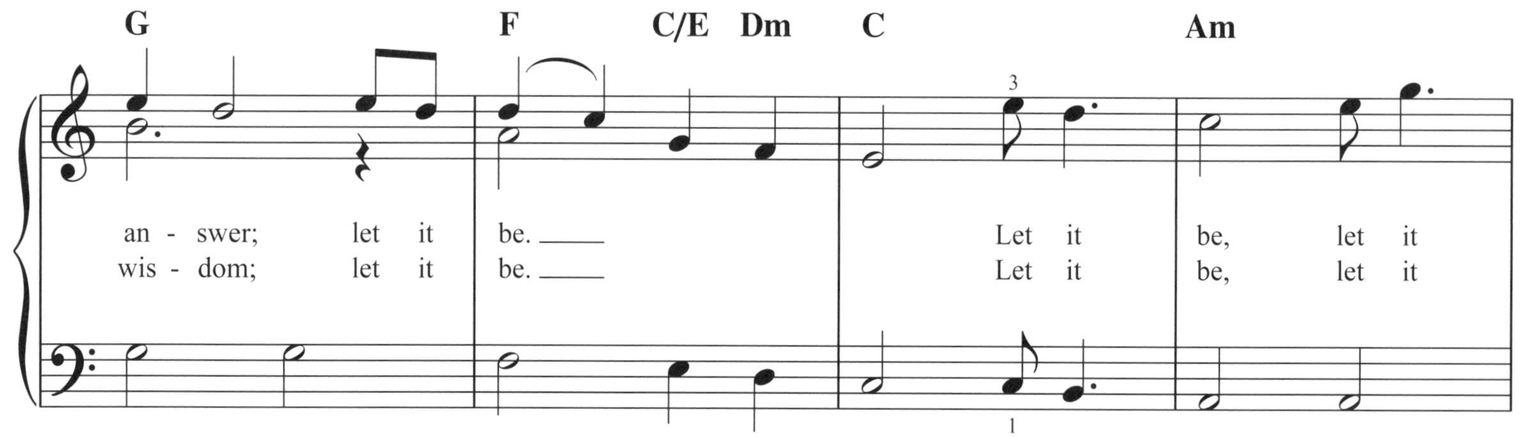
G
F
C/E
Dm
C
Am
an - swer; let it be. Let it be, let it
wis - dom; let it be. Let it be, let it

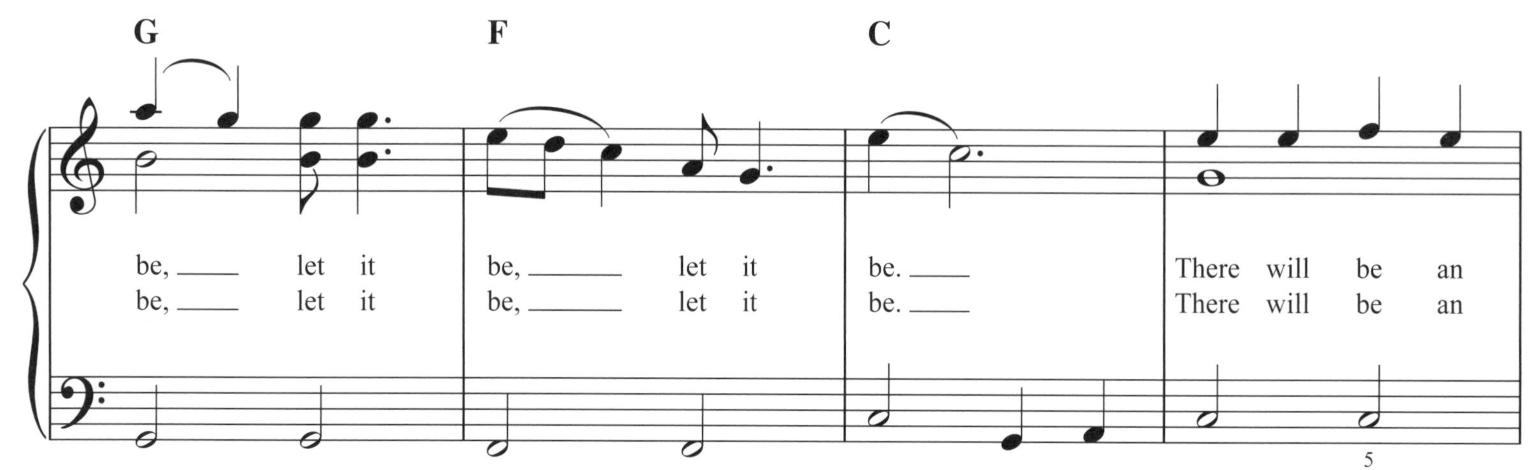
G
F
C
be, let it be, let it be. There will be an
be, let it be, let it be. There will be an

G
F
C/E
Dm
C
Am
an - swer; let it be. Let it be, let it
an - swer; let it be. Let it be, let it
G
F
C
be, let it be, let it be. Whis - per words of
be, let it be, let it be. There will be an
G
F
C/E
Dm
C
N.C.
wis - dom; let it be.
an - swer; let it be.
(like a hymn)
1.
C
2.
C

THE LONG AND WINDING ROAD

Words and Music by JOHN LENNON
and PAUL McCARTNEY

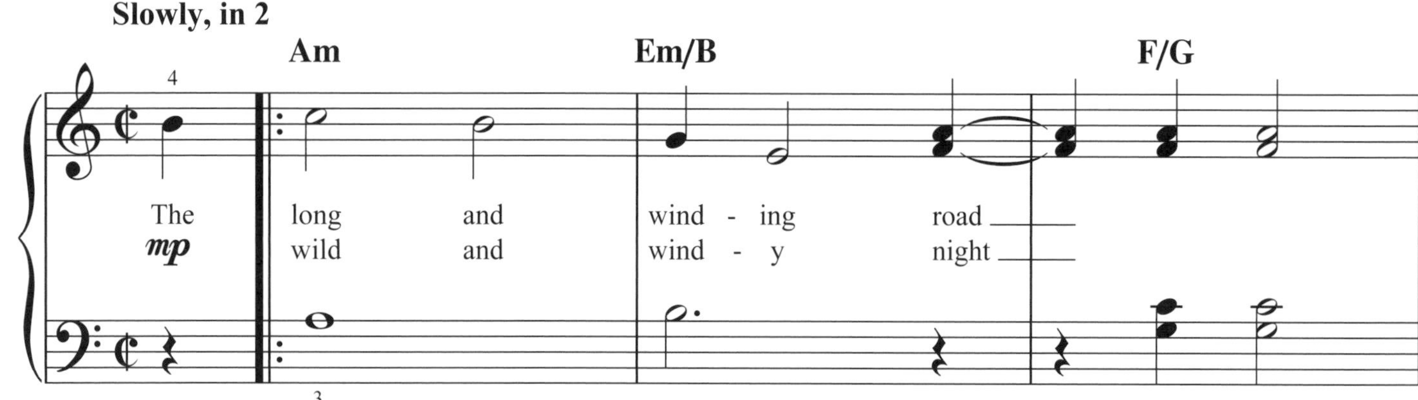

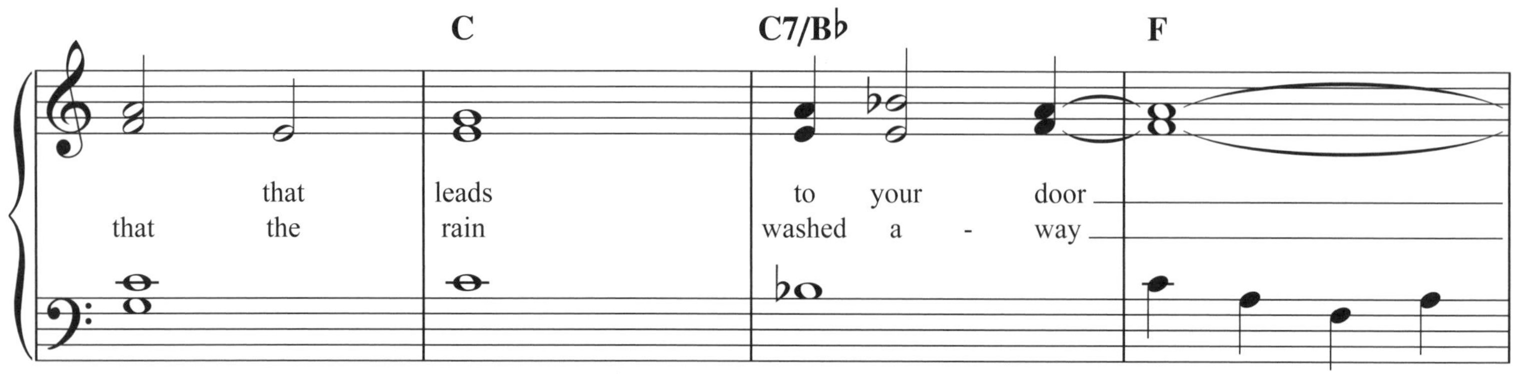

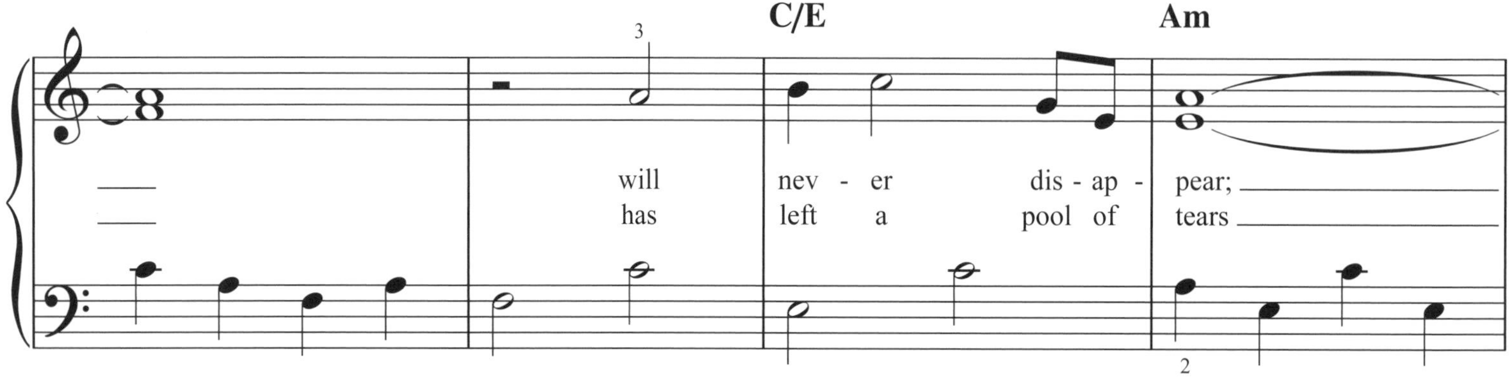

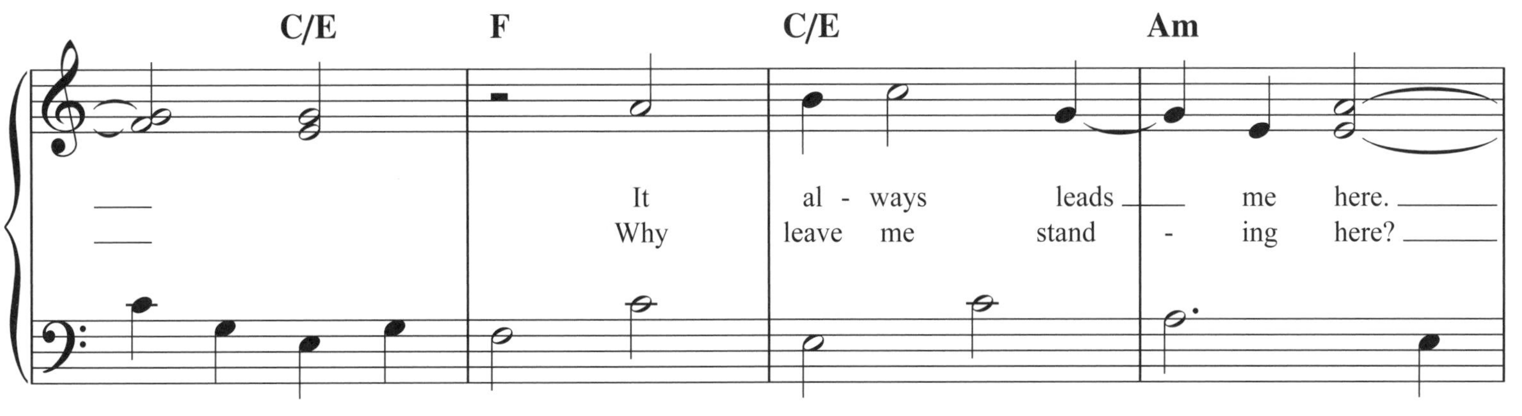
C/E
F
C/E
Am
It al - ways leads me here.
Why leave me stand - ing here?

Dm7
G7
1.
C
Lead me to your door.
Let me know the

2.
C
C/G
The way.
Man - y times I've

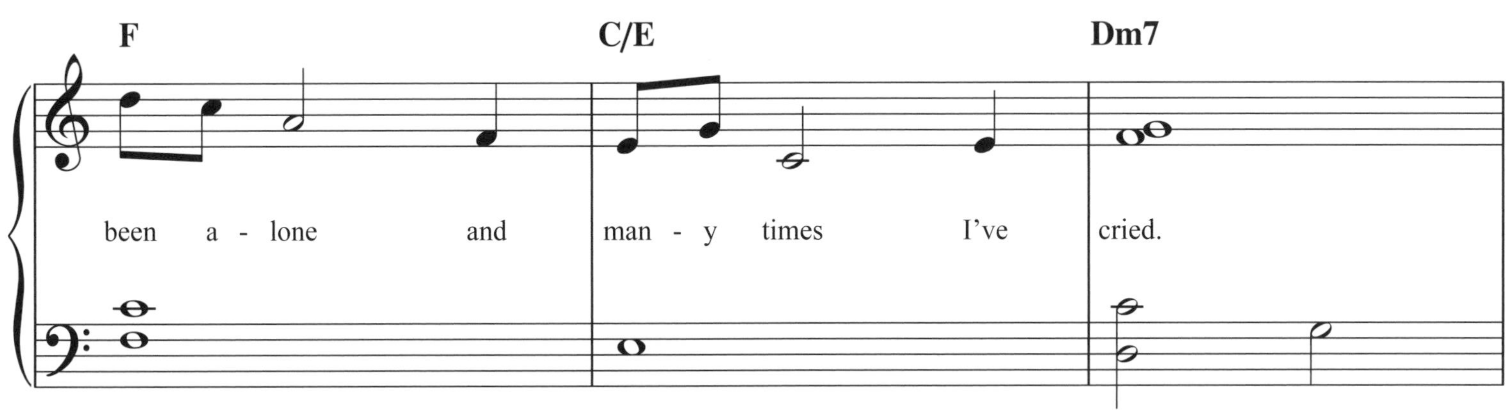
F
C/E
Dm7
been a - lone and man - y times I've cried.

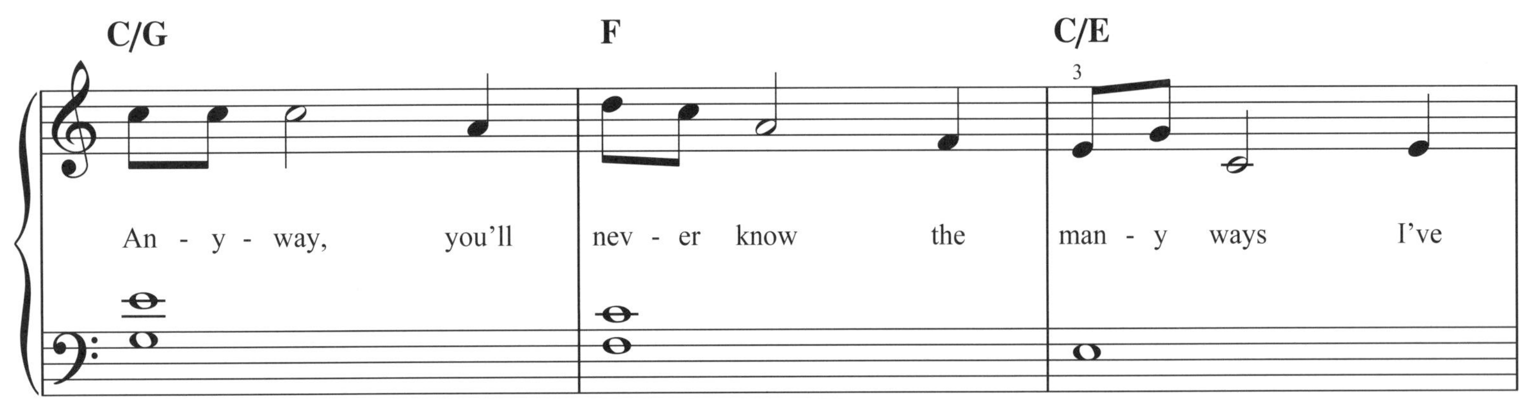
C/G
F
C/E
3
An - y - way, you'll
nev - er know the
man - y ways I've

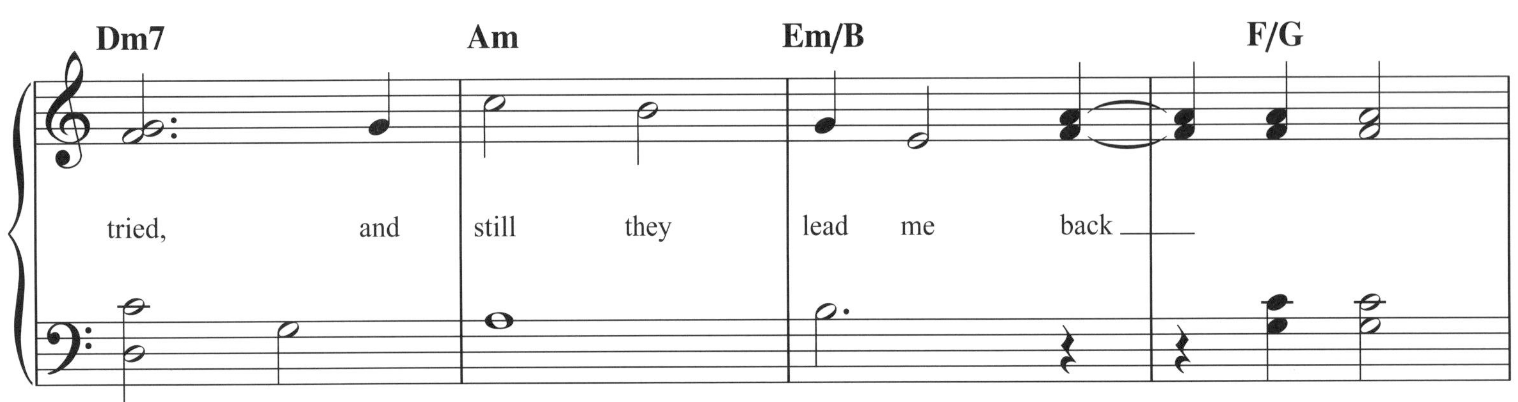
Dm7
Am
Em/B
F/G
tried, and
still they
lead me back

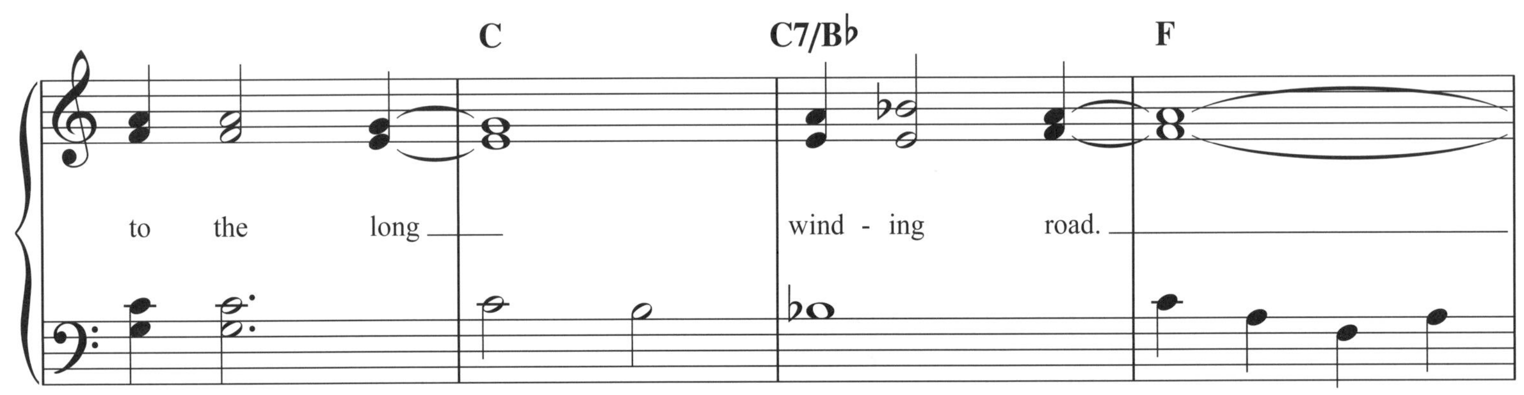
C
C7/B♭
F
to the long
wind - ing road.

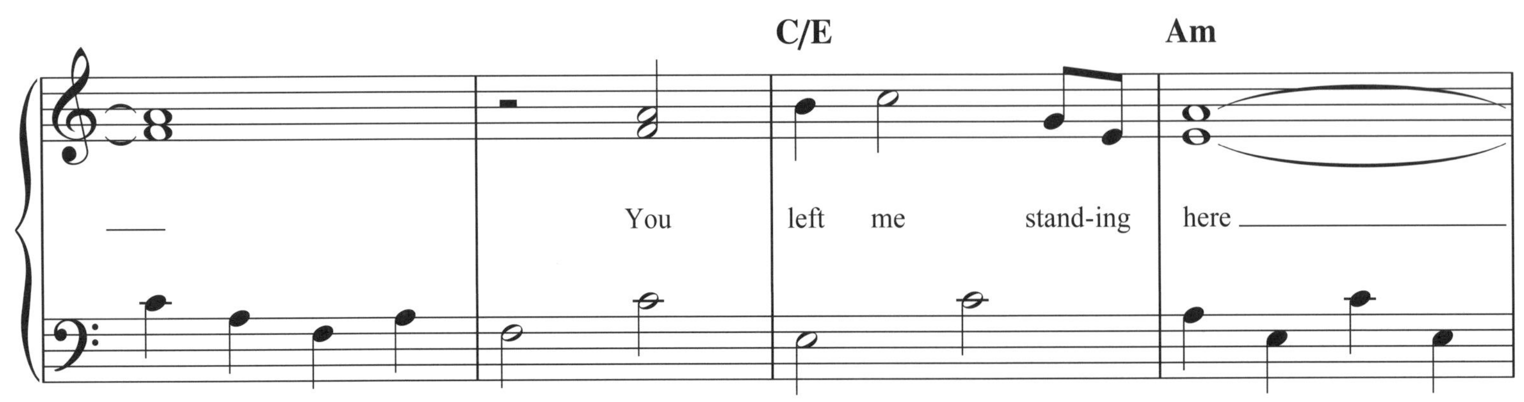
C/E
Am
You
left me stand-ing
here

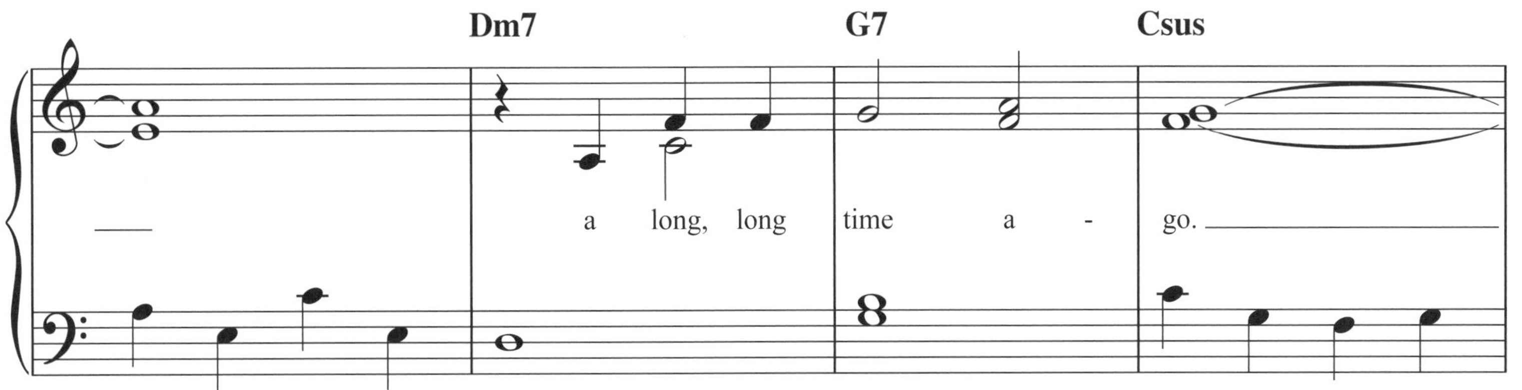
Dm7
G7
Csus
a long, long time a - go.

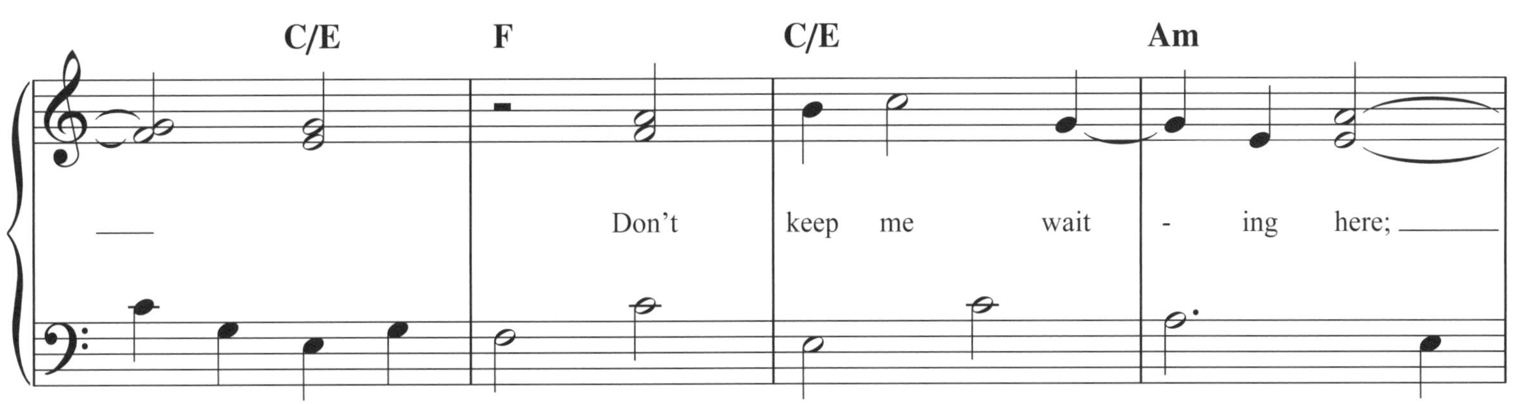
C/E
F
C/E
Am
Don't keep me wait - ing here;

Dm7
G7
Am
lead me to your door.

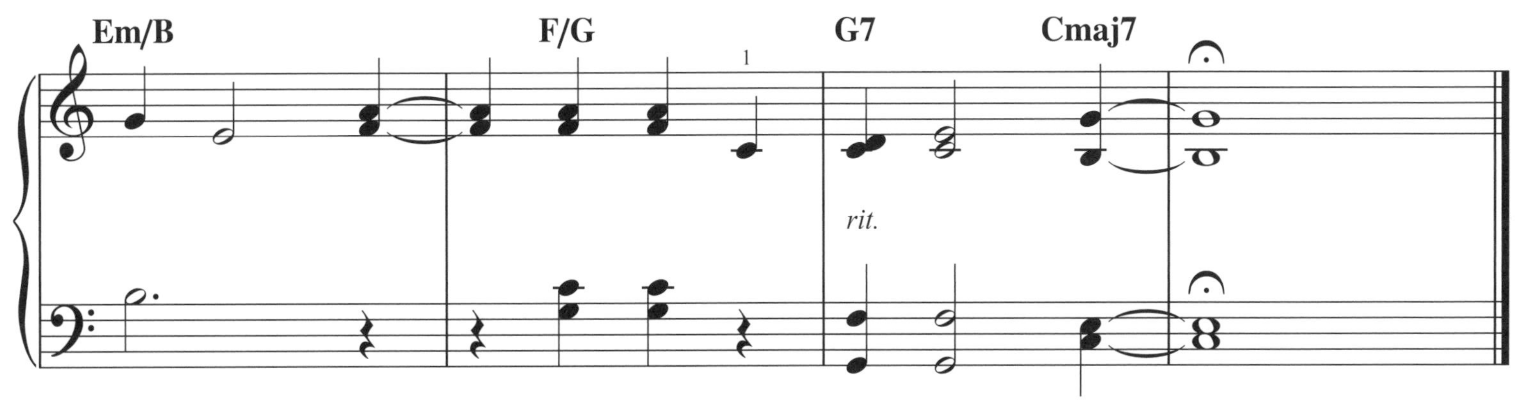
Em/B
F/G
G7
Cmaj7
rit.

OB-LA-DI, OB-LA-DA

Words and Music by JOHN LENNON
and PAUL McCARTNEY

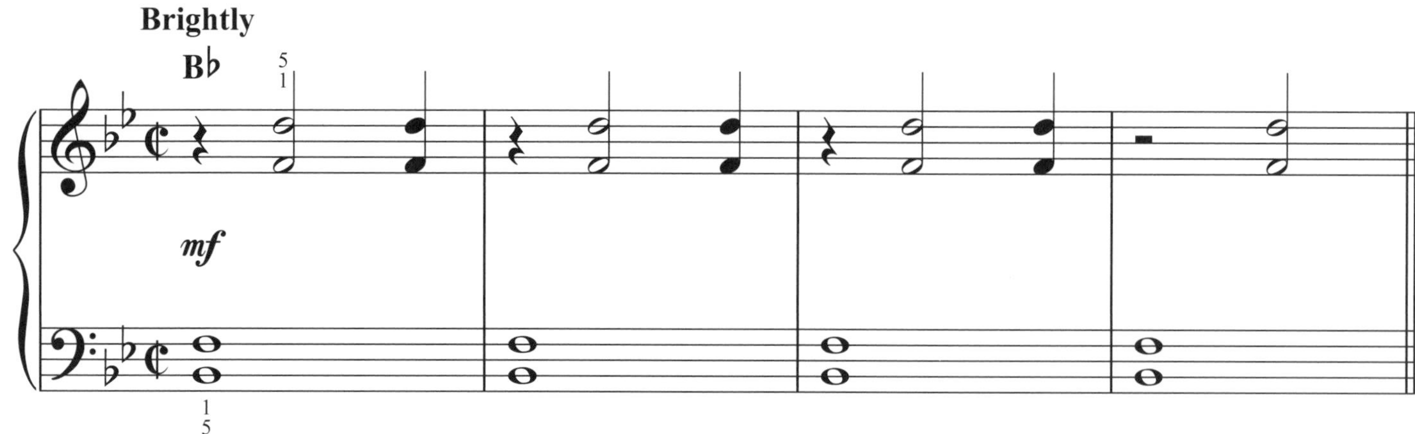

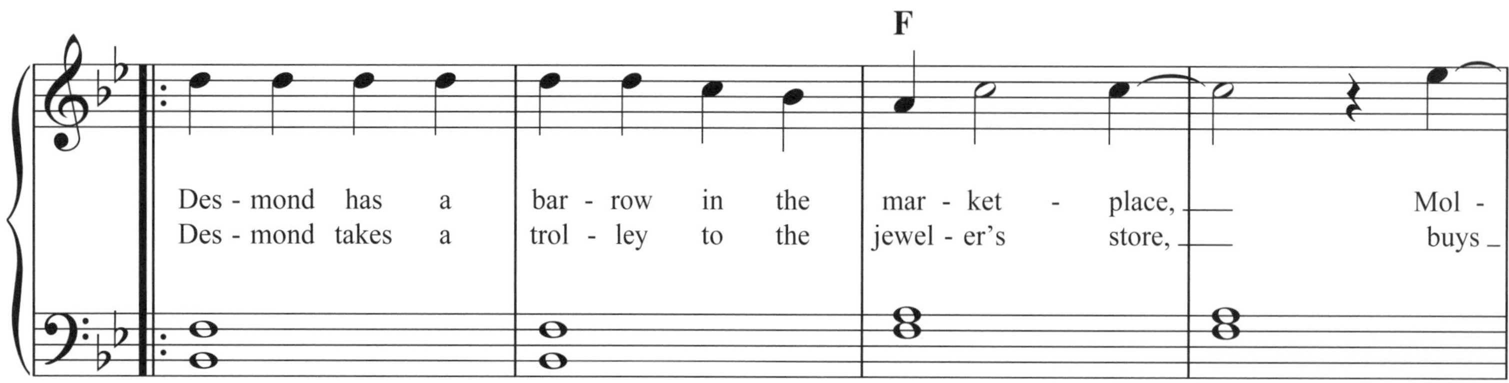

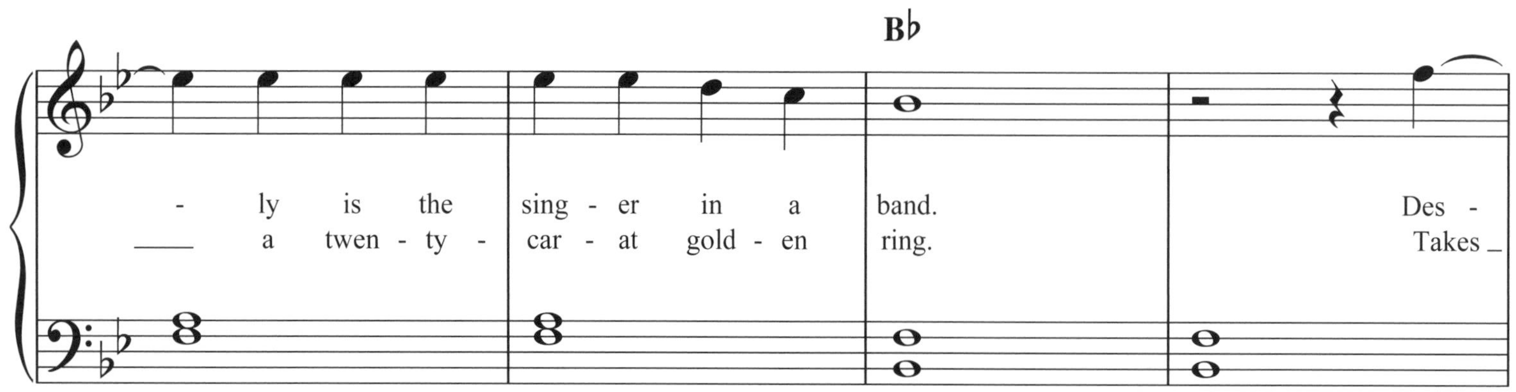

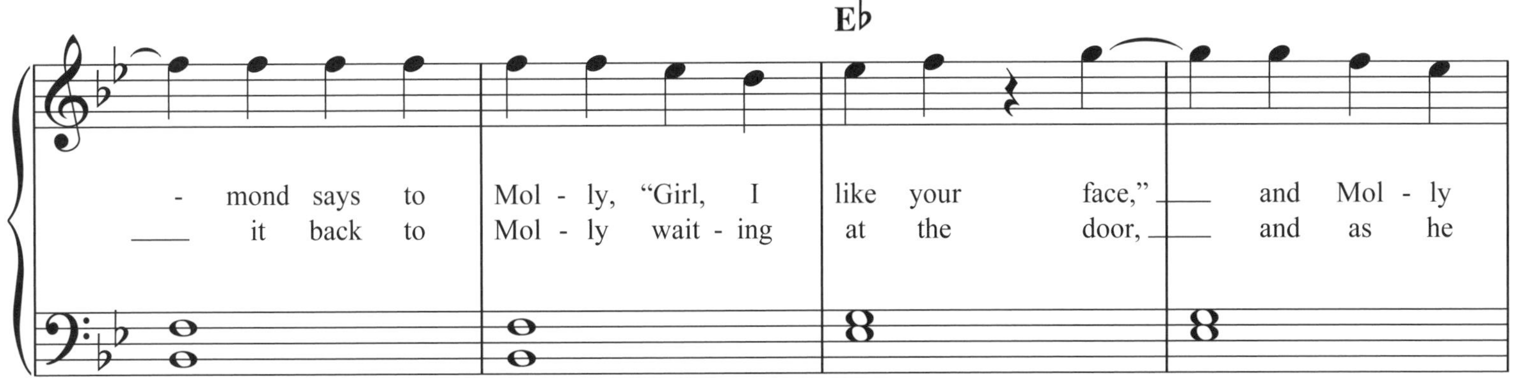
E♭
- mond says to Mol - ly, "Girl, I like your face," and Mol - ly
it back to Mol - ly wait - ing at the door, and as he

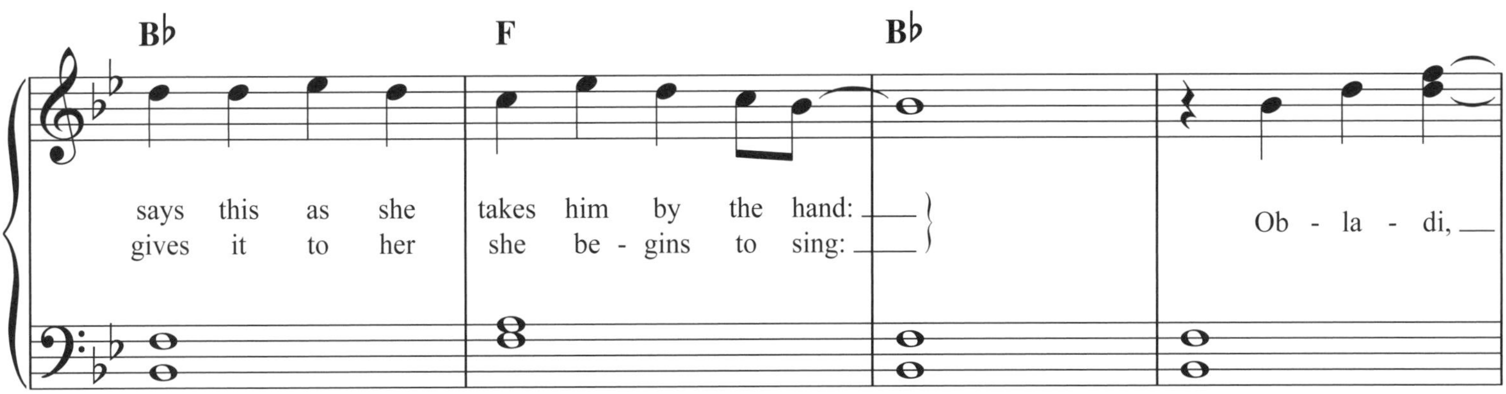
B♭ F B♭
says this as she takes him by the hand:
gives it to her she be - gins to sing:
Ob - la - di,

Dm Gm
ob - la - da, life goes on, bra, la,

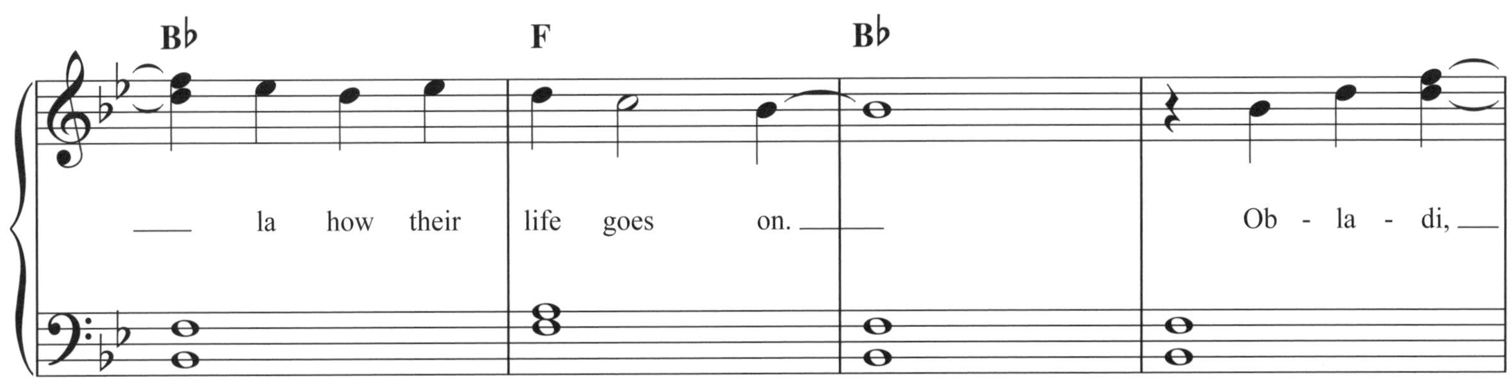
B♭ F B♭
la how their life goes on. Ob - la - di,

Dm
Gm
ob - la - da,
life goes on,
bra,
la,

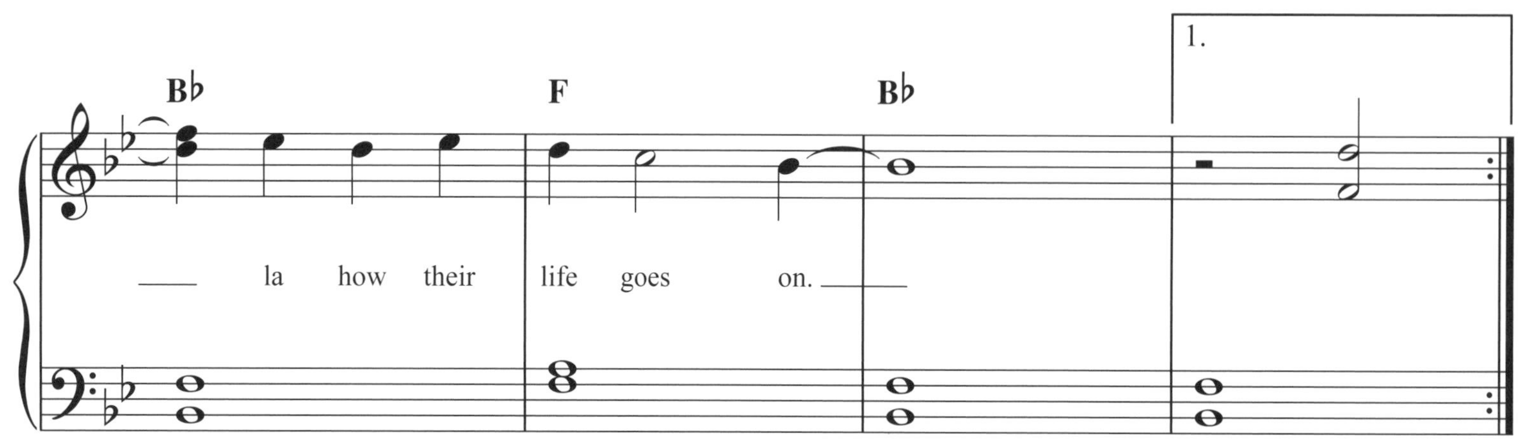
B♭
F
B♭
1.
la how their
life goes
on.

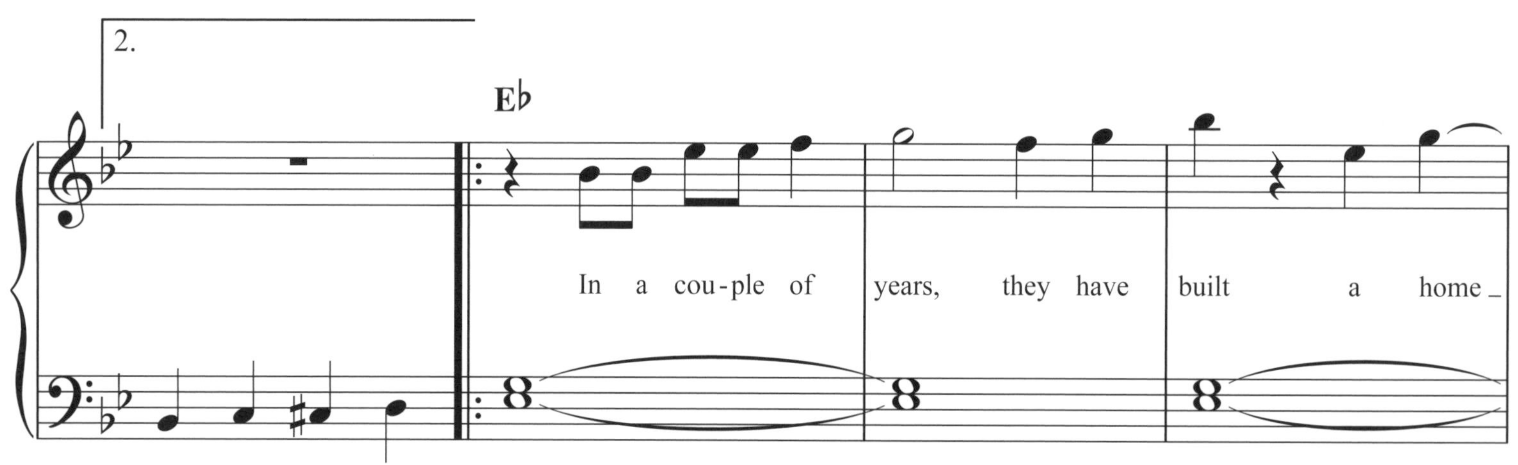
2.
E♭
In a cou-ple of
years, they have
built a home

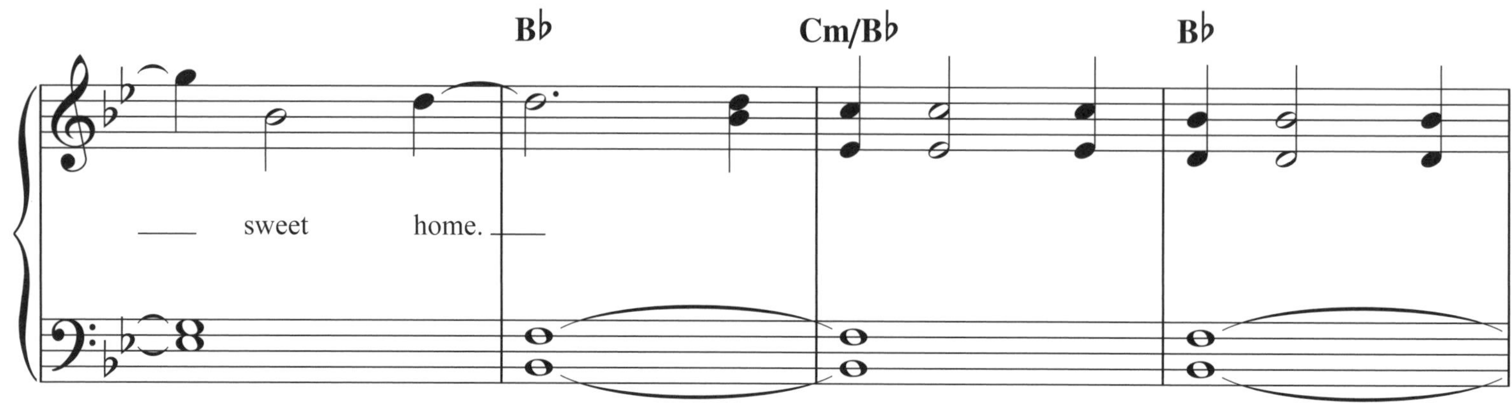
B♭
Cm/B♭
B♭
sweet home.

Bb9
Eb
With a cou-ple of kids run - ning in the yard

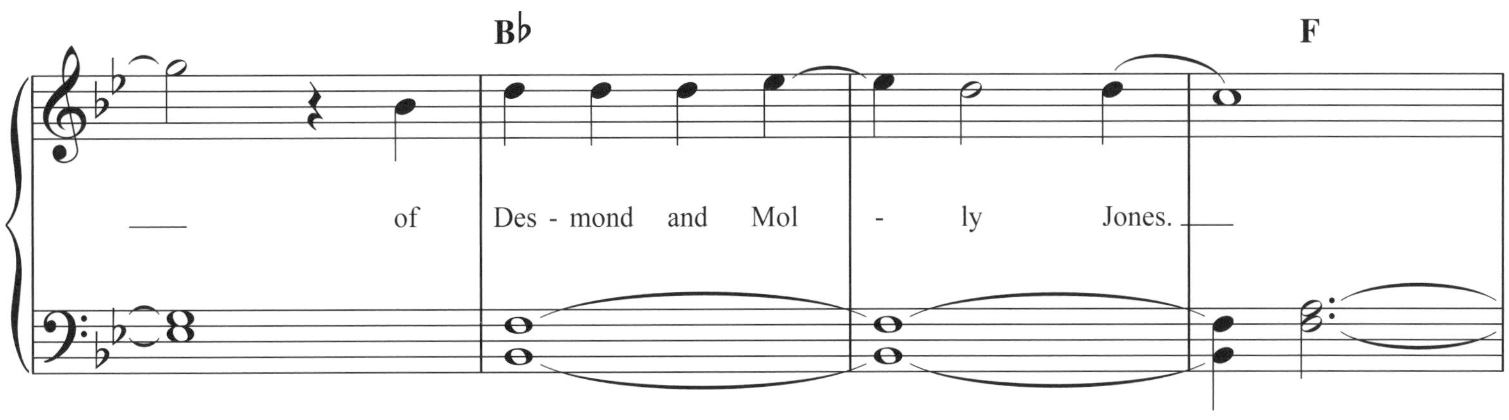
Bb
F
of Des - mond and Mol - ly Jones.

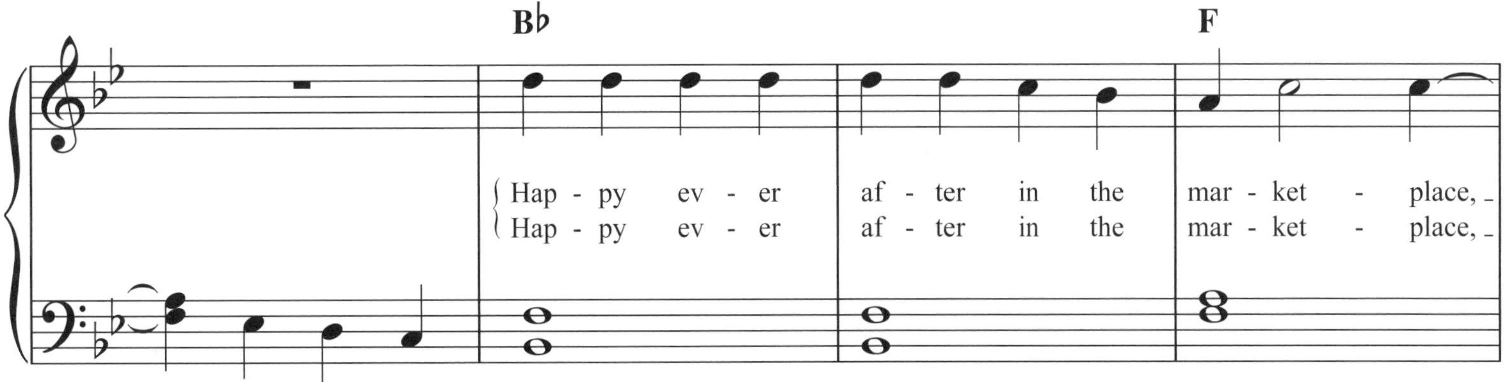
Bb
F
Hap - py ev - er af - ter in the mar - ket - place,
Hap - py ev - er af - ter in the mar - ket - place,

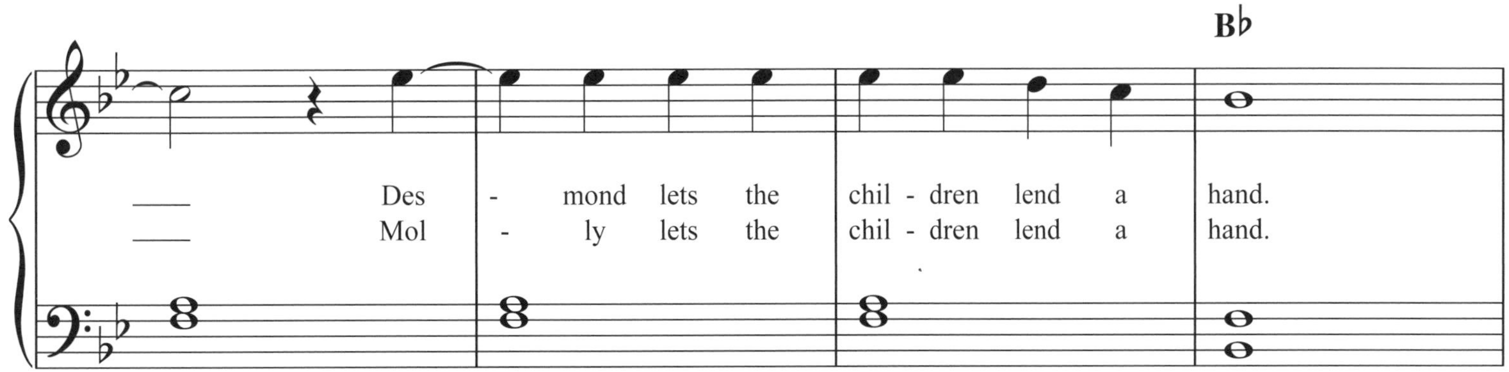
Bb
Des - mond lets the chil - dren lend a hand.
Mol - ly lets the chil - dren lend a hand.

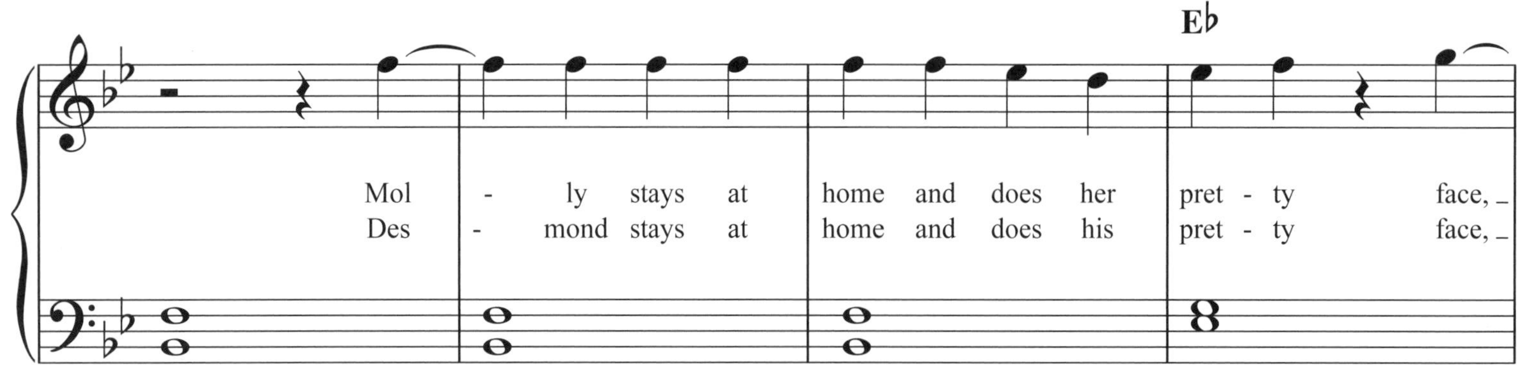
E♭
Mol - ly stays at home and does her pret - ty face, _
Des - mond stays at home and does his pret - ty face, _

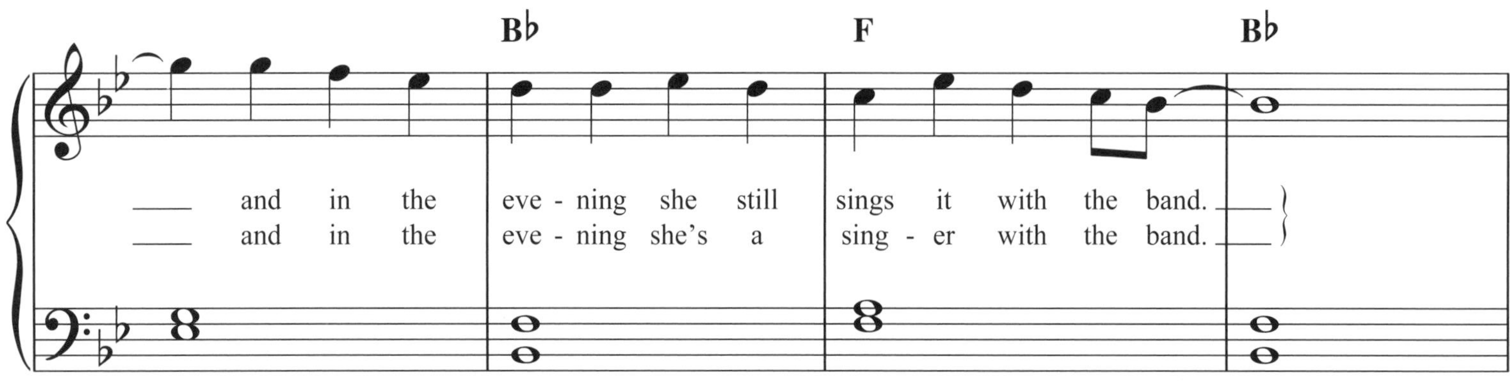
B♭
F
B♭
_ and in the eve - ning she still sings it with the band. _
_ and in the eve - ning she's a sing - er with the band. _

Dm
Ob - la - di, _ ob - la - da, _ life goes on, _ bra, _

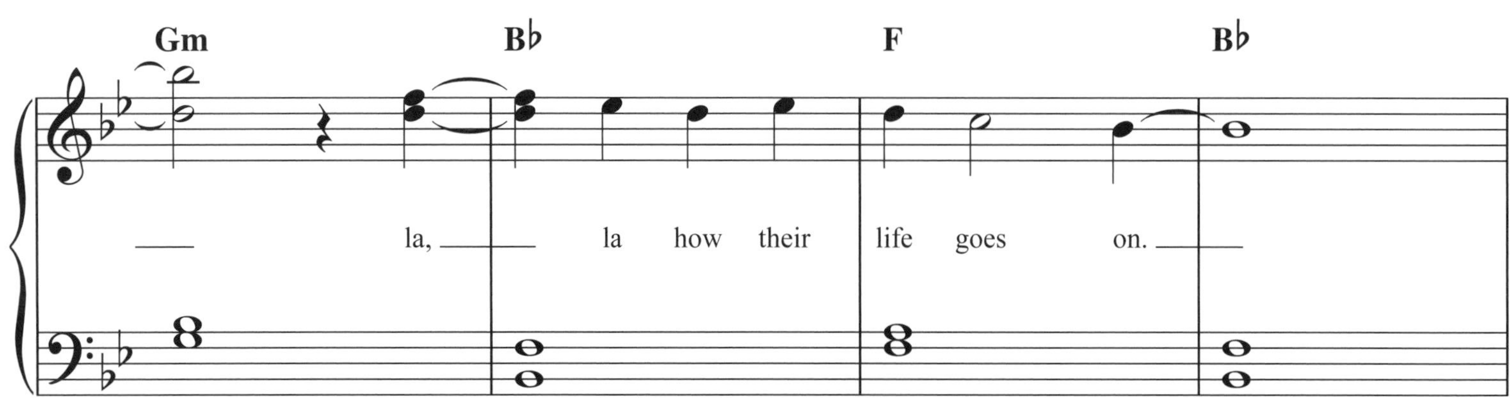
Gm
B♭
F
B♭
_ la, _ la how their life goes on. _

Dm
Ob - la - di,
ob - la - da,
life goes on,
bra,

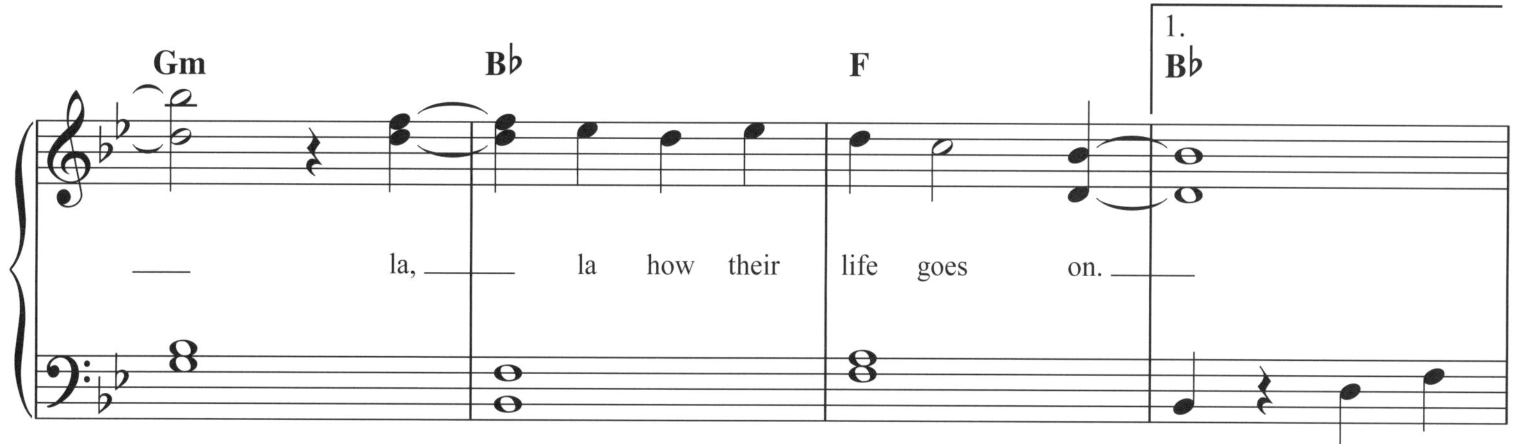
Gm
B♭
F
1.
B♭
la,
la how their
life goes
on.

2.
Gm
And if you
want some fun,

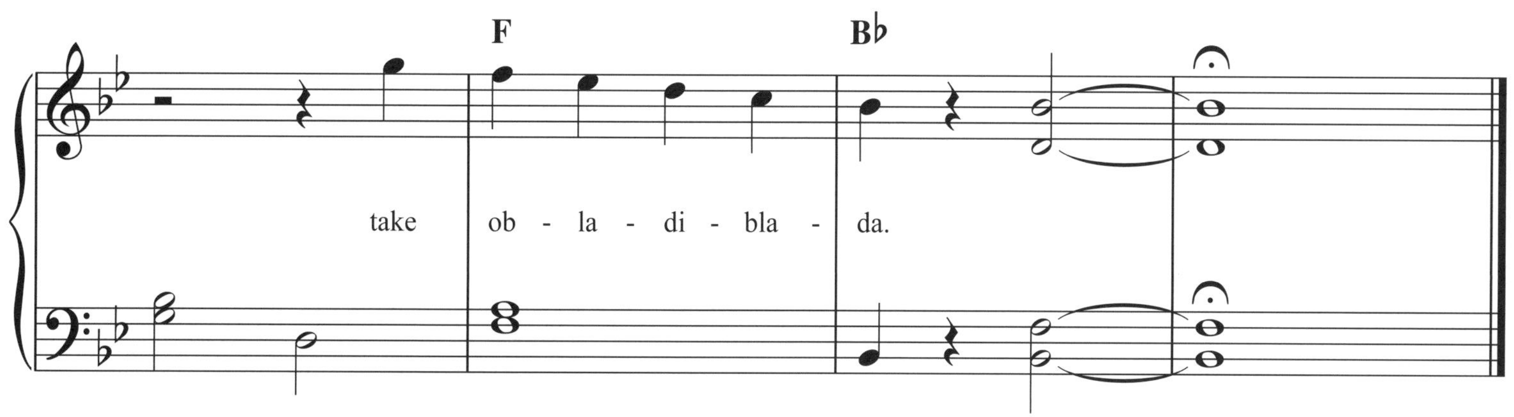
F
B♭
take
ob - la - di - bla -
da.

SHE LOVES YOU

Words and Music by JOHN LENNON
and PAUL McCARTNEY

C
F
say:
She says she
loves you and you
know that can't be

Dm
B♭m/F
bad.
Yes, she
loves you and you
know you should be

C
F
Dm7
glad.
She
said you hurt her
know it's up to
so,
you,
she
I

Am
C
F
al - most lost her
think it's on - ly
mind.
fair.
But
now she says she
Pride can hurt you

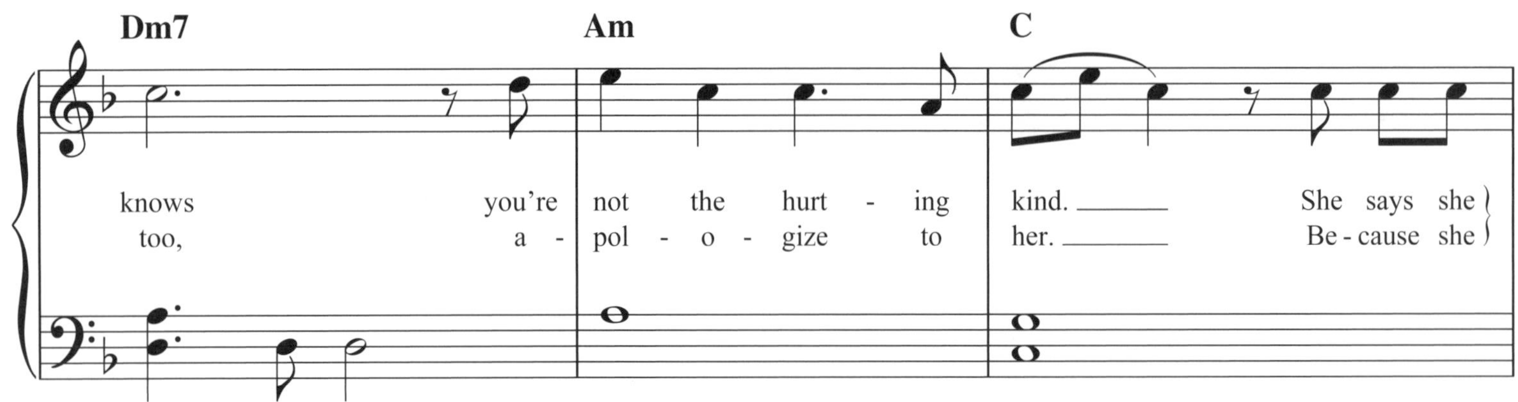
Dm7
Am
C
knows you're not the hurt - ing kind.
too, a - pol - o - gize to her.
She says she
Be - cause she

F
Dm
3
2
loves you and you know that can't be bad.
Yes, she

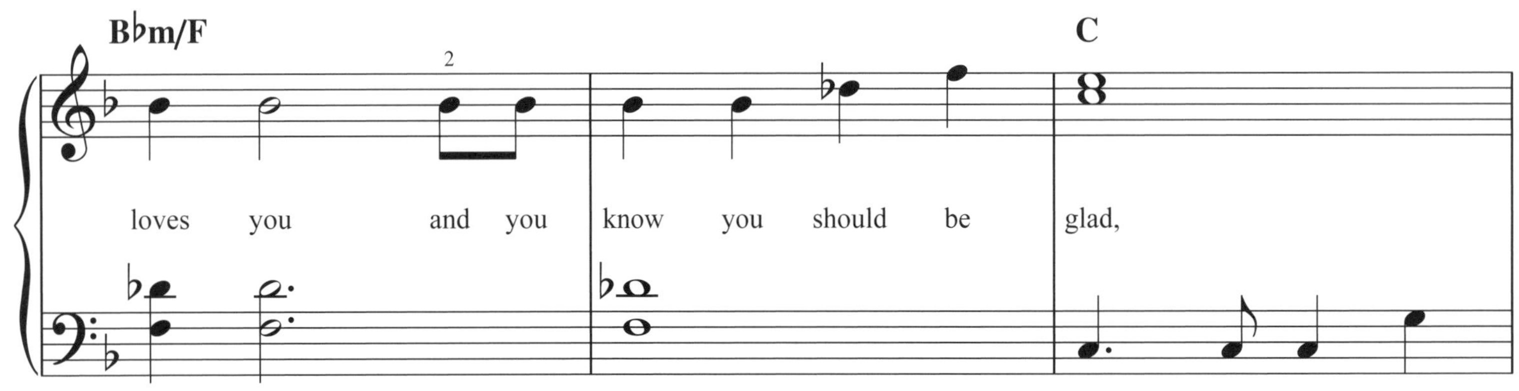
B♭m/F
C
2
loves you and you know you should be glad,

Dm
G7
oo! She loves you, yeah, yeah, yeah, she loves you, yeah,

B♭m/F
C
yeah, yeah. And with a love like that you know you should be

1.
2.
F
F
glad. You
glad. With a

B♭m/F
C
In tempo
F
love like that you know you should be glad. Yeah, yeah, yeah,
slowing
much slower

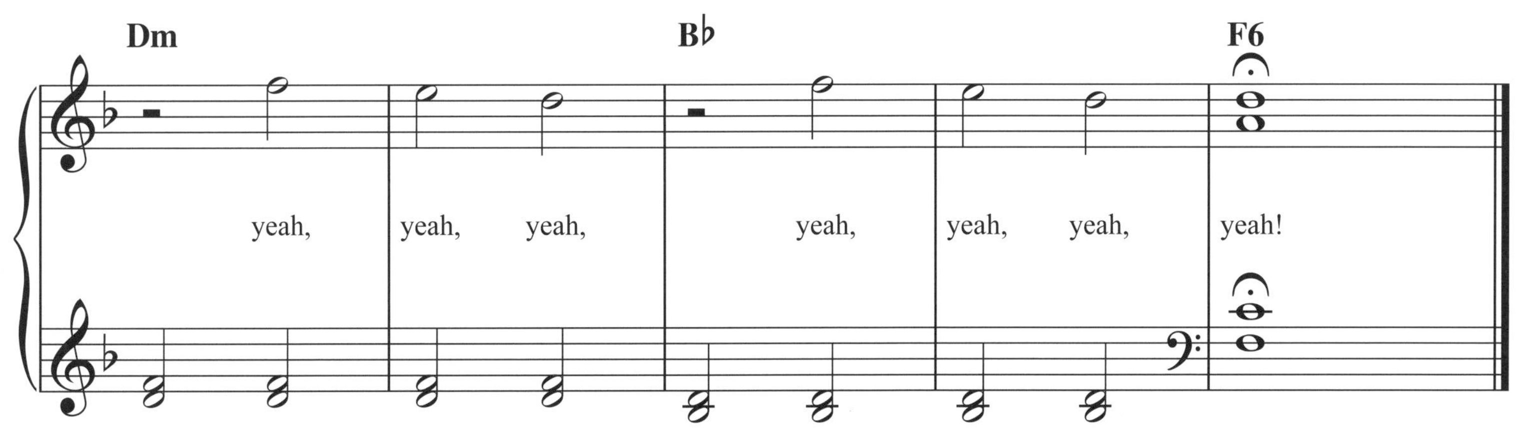
Dm
B♭
F6
yeah, yeah, yeah, yeah, yeah, yeah, yeah!

YESTERDAY

Words and Music by JOHN LENNON
and PAUL McCARTNEY

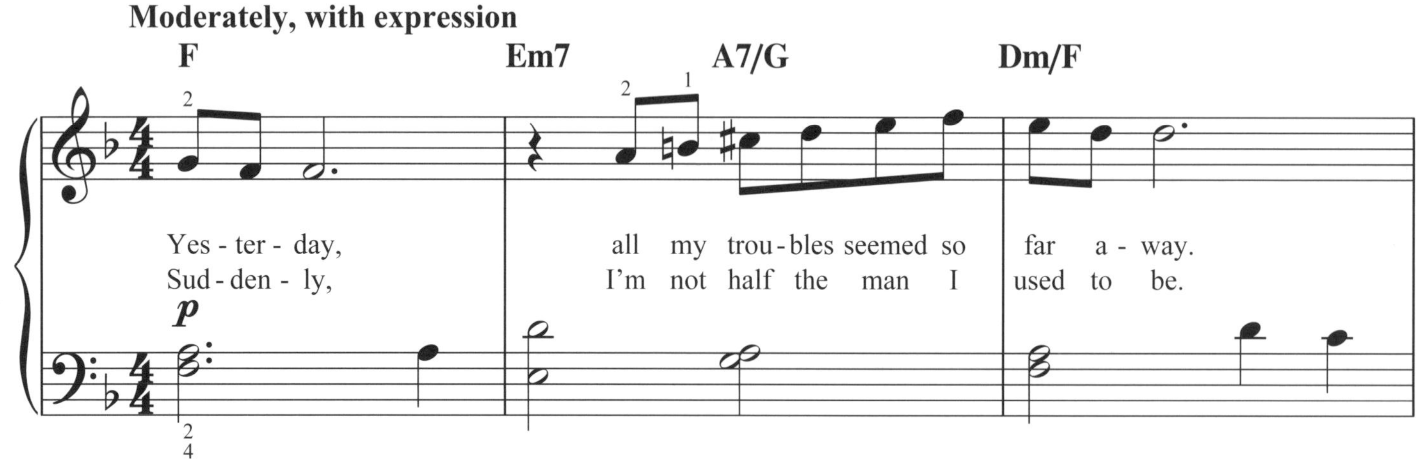

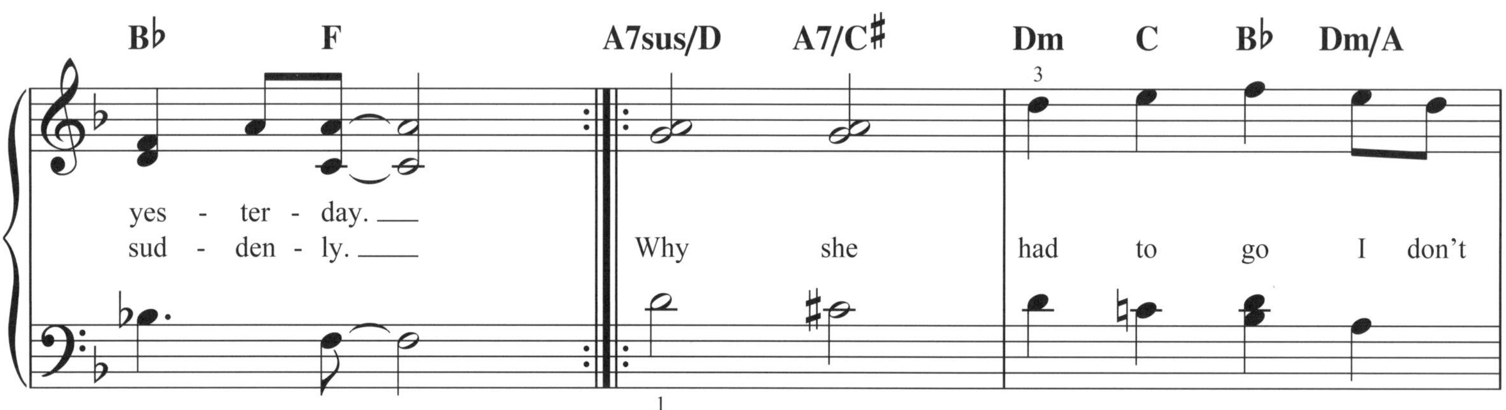

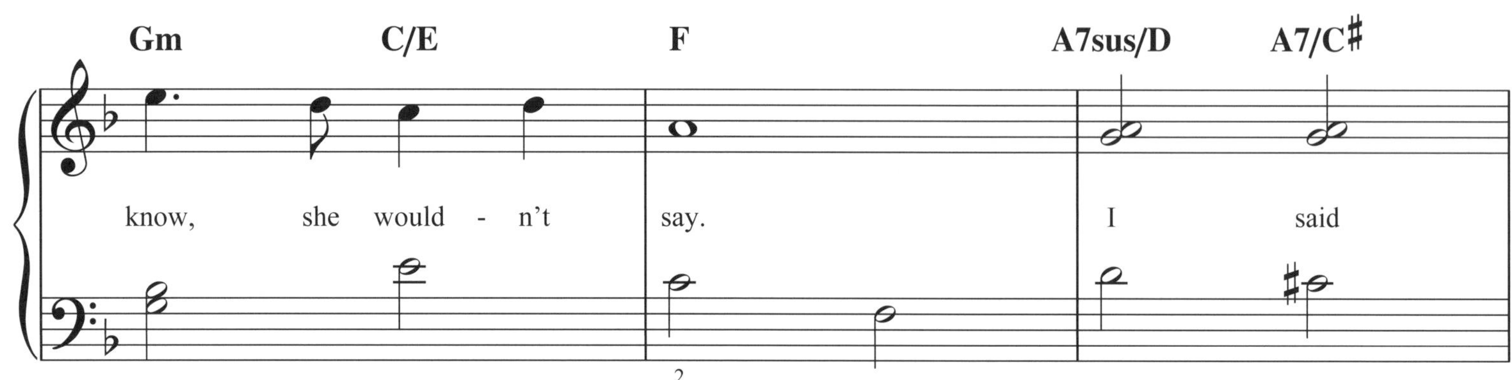

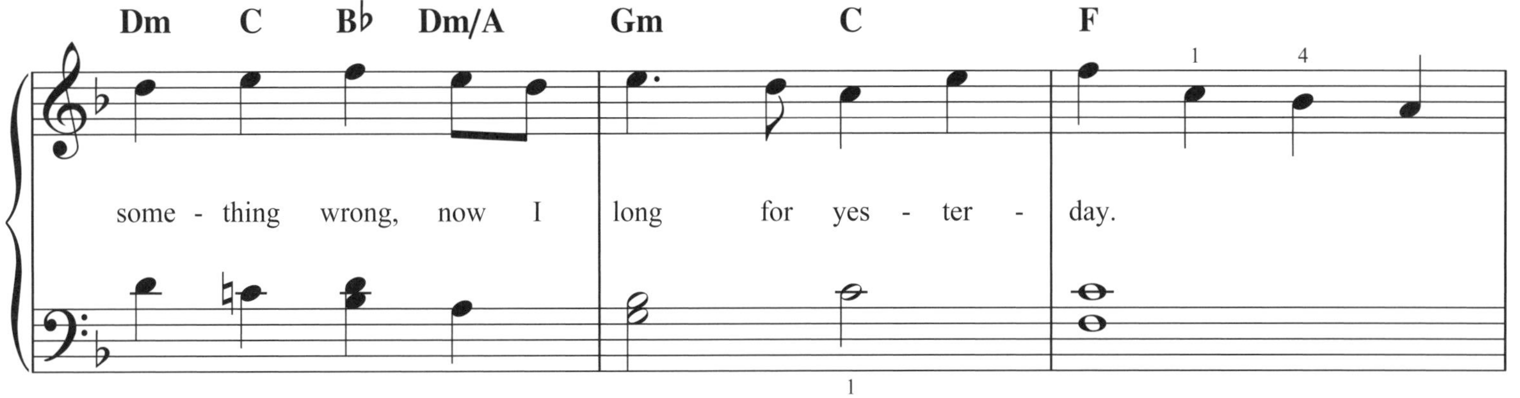
Dm C B♭ Dm/A Gm C F
some - thing wrong, now I long for yes - ter - day.

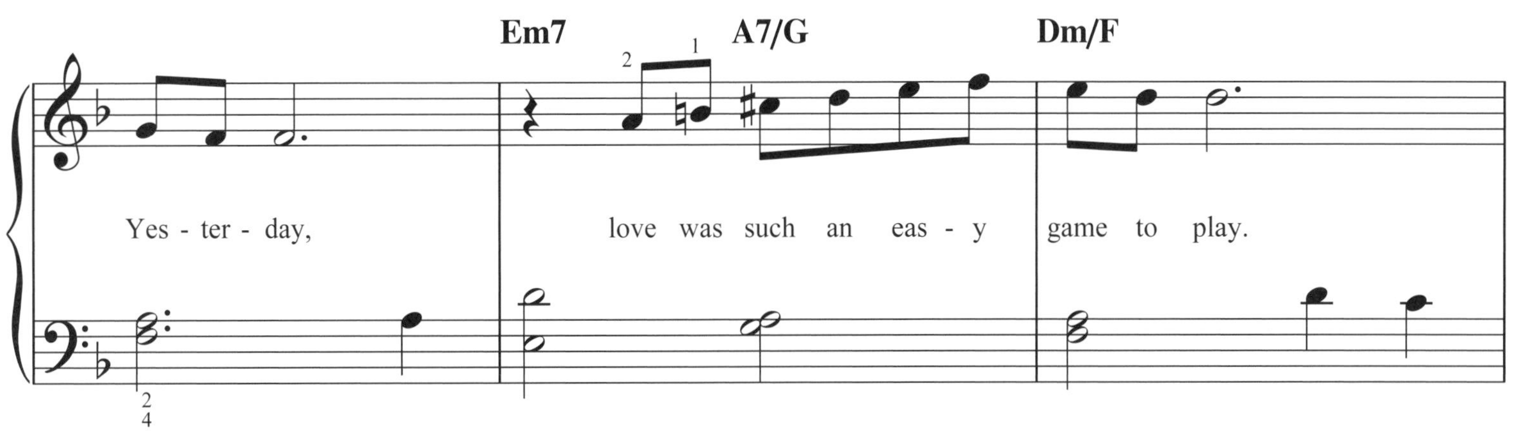
Em7 A7/G Dm/F
Yes - ter - day, love was such an eas - y game to play.

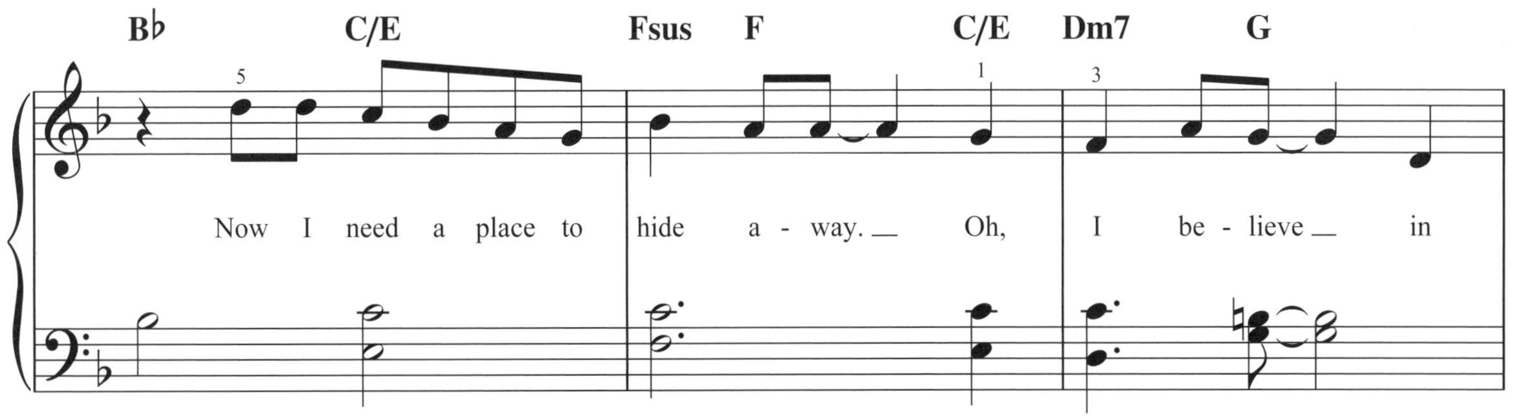
B♭ C/E Fsus F C/E Dm7 G
Now I need a place to hide a - way. Oh, I be - lieve in

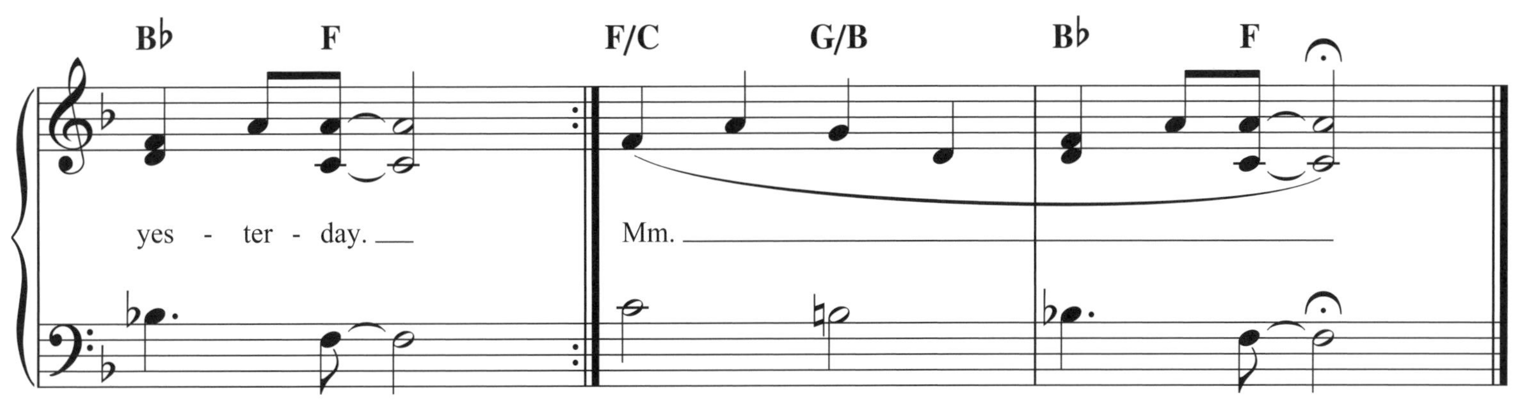
B♭ F F/C G/B B♭ F
yes - ter - day. Mm.